Treasure C
for
Public Speaking

witticisms wisecracks wordplay quips

Treasure Chest
for
Public Speaking

witticisms wisecracks wordplay quips

Terry O'Brien

Rupa & Co

Typeset by
Anvi Composers
19, A1-B, DDA Market
Paschim Vihar
New Delhi 110 063

Printed in India by
Shree Maitrey Printech Pvt. Ltd.
A-84, Sector-2
Noida-201301

*I dedicate this book to late Prof. A. P. O'Brien,
my father, friend, guide and mentor, who
inspired me to the canon of excellence:
re-imagining what's essential*

PREFACE

It is imperative that while public speaking one is well – prepared with stimulating impromptu remarks! It is inexcusable for a speaker to be dull. This book is meant to be a practical, helpful reference book not only for toastmasters, but also for lawyers, teachers, salespersons, businessmen, ministers and those in public life who are called on frequently or occasionally for brief remarks. General readers will find humour, wisdom and inspiration in items that the book contains.

As a public broadcaster for both the audio and visual media and an anchor, compere and a motivational speaker, I have built this collection to share with my readers.

Happy reading
Qizzically yours

Terry O'Brien

EPIGRAMS AND WITTICISM

* An optimistic gardener is a person who believes that what goes down must come up
* A luxury is something you don't need but feel you can't do without
* The fellow who embezzles the money always seems calm and collected
* The family that isn't in debt today is underprivileged
* When you go on a vacation to forget everything, you generally find when you open your bag at the hotel that you have
* Early to bed and early to rise, and you'll miss hearing and seeing a great deal that would make you wise
* Travel flattens the purse, broadens the mind, and lengthens the conversation
* Most girls prefer the strong, solvent type
* Some persons are the kind of friends who stand by you-with their arms folded
* By the time you get enough experience to be able to watch your step, you may not be going anywhere
* More people would try to do right if they thought it was wrong
* Solomon said, " There is no new thing under the sun," but he didn't say it over colour television
* Some people do not just believe what they hear but repeat it
* The reason the road to success is crowded is that it is filled with women pushing their husbands
* You can measure the progress of civilization by who gets more applause - the clown or the thinker
* Time is what passes between paydays
* On a bus there is no such thing as the rising generation
* A cat doesn't have nine lives, but catty remarks do
* Work is time you spend on jobs you get paid for, and leisure is time you spend on jobs you don't get paid for
* A fellow who watches the clock need not worry about his future because he probably hasn't any
* He who laughs last must have time to waste
* Your best friends are generally those you don't meet very often

* By the time you save enough so you can sleep late in the morning, you're so old you want to get up early
* Life is pretty simple - you only need a comfortable bed and comfortable shoes, because you are in one or the other all your life
* A reckless driver may get to places a little sooner - even the cemetery
* You have to be nice until you earn your first million, and after that folks will be nice to you
* Modern youngsters are precocious. They don't read, but name any CD and they can tell what's next in order
* A man's hair is either parted or departed
* The hardest rupee to earn is the one you have already spent
* The person who leaves becomes the life of the party
* Underprivileged: Not to have a remote control for your colour television
* After an election speech, the audience draws its own confusions
* It's what guests say after they say good night that counts
* The only thing that gives you more for your money today than it did a year ago is a weighing machine
* Nothing stretches slacks like snack
* Courage is what it takes to stand up and speak; courage is also what it takes to sit down and listen
* The world is composed of givers and takers. The takers may eat better, but the givers sleep better
* The beginning of wisdom is silence. The second step is listening
* Early to bed and early to rise - till you make enough cash to do otherwise
* The trouble with people these days is that they want to reach the promised land without going through the wilderness
* If you look like your passport photo, you aren't well enough to travel
* If the knocking at the door is loud and long, it isn't opportunity, it's relatives
* The best way to lose weight is to leave it on the plate
* When life knocks you on your knees, you're in a position to pray

★ There's a book that tells you where to go on your vacation. It's called your cheque book
★ There's one advantage to the music the younger generation goes for today: nobody can whistle it.
★ People are peculiar - they want the front of the bus, the back of the church, and the middle of the road
★ When you sing your own praises, it's generally a solo
★ Most wallets wouldn't be so fat today if you took out the credit cards
★ If you want more leisure, get to your appointments on time
★ You can stand still and watch the world go by - and it certainly will
★ No dreams come true until you wake up and go to work
★ By the time you get the instalments paid, the luxury you bought is a necessity
★ The world isn't getting smaller. The missiles just go farther
★ One thing about getting old is that you can sing in the bathroom while brushing your teeth
★ No opportunity is lost; the other fellow takes it
★ You can't make trouble for others without a little of it rubbing off on you
★ Three square meals everyday and you will soon be round
★ Making money last is just as hard as making it first
★ A hammer may miss its mark, but a compliment never
★ To get ahead you have to use your head
★ A girl loves a boy's voice when it has a ring in it
★ Today no one is so poor that he has to live within his income
★ Don't worry too much about what people think, because they seldom do
★ The brain seldom wears out, probably because it's seldom overworked
★ The fellow who says the church is losing ground is probably the same one who says the sun is losing heat
★ Some persons are born good and others have to make good
★ In the grammatically correct home the wife says, "You shall" and the husband says, "I will"

* If you would like to be talked about, leave the party before the rest do
* When both the speaker and an audience are confused, the speech is profound
* Most women have a skin they love to retouch
* Money has wings and most of us see only the tail feathers
* One way to find out what a woman really thinks of you is to marry her
* Conversation without a touch of scandal gets very dull for most people
* A fisherman is the only person who tells a lie with his arms stretched out
* The most effective answer to an insult is silence
* When some women promise to be on time, it carries a lot of wait
* The way to get in *Who's Who* is to know what's what
* People who live in glass houses have to answer the doorbell
* The longer you carry a grudge, the heavier it gets
* The happiest moment in your life is when folks back of you in the *movies* finish their popcorn
* Some persons don't know the difference between thinking for yourself and thinking of yourself
* Worry takes as much time as work and pays less
* Worrying is like a rocking chair - it makes you do something but takes you nowhere
* As you grow older, you grow wiser, talk less, and say more
* It's impossible to keep your mind and your mouth open at the same time
* As a rule, a quitter isn't a very good beginner either
* The straight and narrow path never crosses Easy Street
* We have discovered that women used cosmetics in the Middle Ages. They still use them in the middle ages
* The Christmas cooing is followed by the January billing
* The family that isn't in debt today is underprivileged
* The Bible is such a great book that it survives all the translations made of it
* The world's choice: Disarmament or Disbursement

★ A telephone isn't a vacuum cleaner, but some people can get a lot of dirt out of it

★ No horse goes as fast as the money you bet on him

★ All things come to him who crosses the street without looking

★ Money talks and in most families it's their mother tongue

★ If you know you don't know much, you know more than most people

★ One reason a child must suck his thumb is that he may need it someday

★ It's a smart child who can ask questions his parents can answer

★ The fellow who is a good sport has to lose to prove it

★ The best speech you hear may be from the fellow who keeps his mouth shut

★ Honesty pays, but not enough to satisfy people

★ You can live a quiet life just by living within your income

★ Always put off until tomorrow the things you shouldn't do at all

★ You are young once, but you can be immature all your life

★ A fool and his money can throw parties

★ Nothing grows to a man's stomach like success

★ Sin is an old-fashioned word used to describe what is now called sophistication

★ Half the world is always ready to tell the other half how to live

★ As you grow older, you stand for more and fall for less

★ When a person is always right, there is something wrong

★ Late to bed and early to rise makes you stupid rather than wise

★ One way to reduce blood pressure is to live within your income

★ The ant may be industrious, but it doesn't get on to the front page as often as the butterfly

★ Truth in advertising: "The latest in antiques"

★ Schooldays are the happiest days that parents have

★ A husband may read his wife like a book, but he can't shut her up that easily

* A generation ago most men who finished a hard day's work needed rest; now they need exercise
* There are five thousand languages and dialects in the world, and money speaks all of them
* A person who is overweight is living beyond his seams
* What the world needs is not people to rewrite the Bible, but people to re-read it
* There are many great books now on how to live longer, but none on why
* A smart husband doesn't go home and complain about dinner, but takes his wife to a restaurant where they can both complain
* No man with money is short of cousins
* Most of us spend a great deal of time letting off esteem
* To reach a great height a person needs to have depth
* Think - and you will be very lonely
* Always put off until tomorrow what you are going to make a mess of today
* It's one thing to guarantee free speech in a country, but it's another thing to guarantee its quality
* Vacation is the period when you spend two weeks in an old shack without conveniences so you can go back to your home with its comforts and complain
* The way to be successful is to follow the advice you give others
* Blessed are the peacemakers - they will never be unemployed
* Believe only one half you hear, but be sure it's the right half
* Most politician candidates are more candied than candid
* Time is a great healer, but it's not much of a beauty parlour
* Some prayers are so long because a person prays for more than he works for
* A small town is a place where a person with a black eye can't say he ran into the door
* Matrimony is a process by which the grocer acquires an account the florist had

* If you punch a man on his nose when he calls you a fool, it may prove he was
* It's bad manners to talk when your mouth is full or your head is empty
* The way to win friends is to lose arguments
* Every time someone makes his mark in the world, someone is waiting to use the erasure
* At a party the conversation never gets good until a few couples leave
* If everyone thought before he spoke, the world would be almost silent
* The person who says that he trusts no one should include himself
* If you can't think of a smart, snappy retort, a slight yawn is just about good
* The government does not expect to live within its income - only within yours
* The persons who live next door listen to both sides of a family argument
* There are two kinds of people who don't generally say much - quiet people and those who talk
* If you give an automobile driver an inch, he will take half your lane
* An intellectual person is a person who only knows how to spell a word one way
* No one can jump down your throat if you keep your mouth shut
* The earth revolves on its axis, but the nations revolve on their taxes
* Everything comes to him who waits, except the time he lost waiting
* We have everything in a modern kitchen now, except a cook
* Art is long, but artists are generally short
* The emptier the pot, the quicker it boils
* When a woman is pensive she is probably just planning something very expensive
* When a girl marries a hardworking young executive, the thing she misses most after marriage is her husband

* Man is the only creature whose brains tell him he should save for the future, but the squirrels and bees do it a lot better naturally
* One way to reach old age is to quit feeling responsible for the entire world
* Variety is the spice of life, but it is good old monotony that gets the groceries home
* Early to bed and early to rise, it takes lots of credit card to do otherwise
* When you buy something for a song, the accompaniment is probably expensive
* Misfortune is a point of view. Your headache feels good to an aspirin salesman

HUMOROUS AND UNUSUAL DEFINITIONS

* Action: The last resort of those who know not how to dream - Oscar Wilde
* Adolescence: The time when children answer the phone
* After - dinner Speaker: The gust of honour
* Alarm clock: A clock that scares the daylights into you
* Ambition: The last refuge of failure - Oscar Wilde
* Angling: The name given to fishing by people who can't fish - Stephen Leacock
* Antique: Something no one would want if there were two of them
* Applause: The echo of platitude
* Atheist: A man who has no invisible means of support- Bishop Fulton J Sheen
* Auction: A place where, if you aren't careful, you'll get something for nodding
* Bachelor: A fellow who failed to embrace his opportunities
* Bookie: pickpocket who lets you use your own hands - Henry Morgon
* Careful driver: One who just saw the driver ahead of him get a traffic ticket
* Caricature: Rough truth - George Meredith
* Charity; A thing that begins at home and usually stays there - Elbert Hubbard
* Duty: What one expects from others - Oscar Wildee

* Economist: A person who knows tomorrow why the things he said yesterday didn't happen today
* Education: What you get from reading the fine print
  Experience: What you get from not reading it
* Efficiency: The ability to get someone do your job
* Etiquette: Knowing which finger to put in your mouth when you whistle for the waiter
* Executive: A person who never puts off until tomorrow what he can get someone else to do today
* Father: A banker provided by nature - French proverb
* Financial success: An accomplishment that helps you see your relatives frequently
* Flattery: The art of telling another person exactly what he thinks of himself
* Forgetfulness: A form of freedom - Khalil Gibran
* Gambling: The sure way of getting nothing for some thing Wilson Mizner
* Gentleman: A person who "is at a big disadvantage these days"-Kin Hubbard
* Go-getter: A person who gets his elbows on both arms of his theatre seat
* Golf: Another method of beating about the bush
* Gossip: Mouth-to-mouth recitation
* Grudge: The heaviest thing that you can carry
* History: A confused heap of facts - Lord Chesterfield
* Home: Where the heart is - Elbert Hubbard
* Inflation: Merely a drop in the buck
* Intellectual: A person who cannot state a simple fact in simple terms
* Joint checking account: One that lets a wife beat her husband to the draw
* Journalism: History on the run - Thomas Griffith
* June: When girls look at the bride side of life
* Laughter: A tranquillizer with no side effects-Arnold Galsow
* Lawyers: Persons who write a 10,000-word document and call it a brief

* ☆ Laziness: The love of physical calm
* ☆ Logic: The art of going wrong with confidence– Joseph Wood Krutch
* ☆ Manners: Noises you don't make while eating soup
* ☆ Marriage: A mistake every man should make - George Jessel
* ☆ News: The first rough draft of history - Ben Bradlee
* ☆ Night watchmen: Yawn patrol
* ☆ Nostalgia: Recalling the fun without remembering the pain
* ☆ Obstinacy: The strength of the weak-minded
* ☆ Philosophy: Common sense in a dress suit
* ☆ Poetry: The impish attempt to paint the colour of the wind-Maxwell Bodenheim
* ☆ Politics: Getting votes from the poor and campaign funds from the rich by promising to protect each from the other
* ☆ Procrastination: The art of keeping up with yesterday-Don Marquis
* ☆ Republic: A government in which those who don't vote criticise those who are elected
* ☆ Research: Getting things out of many old books never read, and putting them into a new book which no one is going to read
* ☆ Second fiddle: One of the most difficult instruments to play
* ☆ Sceptic: Someone who won't take know for an answer
* ☆ Successful person: One who has to borrow money to pay his income taxes
* ☆ Sweater: A garment a child wears when his mother feels chilly
* ☆ Tears: The noble language of the eyes
* ☆ Tomorrow: The biggest laboursaving device ever invented
* ☆ Unhappiness: Not knowing what we want and killing ourselves to get it
* ☆ Vacation: What we take when we can't take what we are taking any longer
* ☆ Wig: A new top on an old chassis
* ☆ Yawn: A silent shout

A

Ability

* Ability is what will get you to the top if the boss has no daughter.
* We rate ability in men by what they finish, not by what they attempt.
* Ability without ambition is like a car without a motor.
* The remarkable thing about most of us is our ability to live beyond our means.
* Ability is the most important tool in your life.
* There is far more opportunity than there is ability.
* What lies behind us and what lies before us are tiny matters compared to what lies within us.

Achievement

* We rate ability in men by what they finish, not by what they attempt.
* Ability without ambition is like a car without a motor.
* Some fellows dream of worthy accomplishments, while others stay awake and do them.
* You can't make a place for yourself under the sun if you keep sitting in the shade of the family tree.
* There are four steps to accomplishment: Plan purposefully. Prepare prayerfully. Proceed positively. Pursue persistently.
* A man seldom knows what he can do until he tries to undo what he did.
* Every accomplishment, great or small, starts with the right decision, "I'll Try."
* The only thing in life achieved without effort is failure.
* Today's preparation determines tomorrow's achievement.
* Do something. Either lead , follow, or get out of the way!
* Choice, not chance, determines destiny.
* Education is not received. It is achieved.
* Having money and friends is easy. Having friends and no money is an accomplishment.
* To be born a gentleman is an accident—to die one is an accomplishment.
* Happiness is a by-product of achievement.

★ A mistake is proof that someone was at least trying to accomplish something.

Action

★ You can't get anywhere unless you start.

★ Kind actions begin with kind thoughts.

★ Actions speak louder than words — and speak fewer lies.

★ The thing to try when all else fails is again.

★ Just over the hill is a beautiful valley, but you must climb the hill to see it.

★ Do it now! Today will be yesterday tomorrow.

★ Giving it another try is better than an alibi.

★ It's better to look where you're going than to see where you've been.

★ Having a great aim in life is important. So is knowing when to pull the trigger.

★ If you're going to climb, you've got to grab the branches, not the blossoms.

★ The actions of men are the best interpreters of their thoughts.

★ Doing beats stewing.

★ God gives us the ingredients for our daily bread, but He expects us to do the baking.

★ There are three ways to get something done: do it yourself, hire someone to do it, or forbid your kids to do it.

★ Begin where you are. But don't stay where you are.

★ The best time to do something worthwhile is between yesterday and tomorrow.

★ Think what others ought to be like, then start being like that yourself.

★ It's nice to be important, but it's more important to be nice.

★ Many pious people would rather study the Bible than practice what it teaches.

★ It's not the load that breaks you down, it's the way you carry it.

★ Business is like a wheelbarrow—it stands still unless somebody pushes it.

★ Common sense is the knack of seeing things as they are, and doing things as they ought to be done.

★ Those who can — do. Those who can't — criticise.

★ The smallest good deed is better than the grandest intention.

★ We make more enemies by what we say than friends by what we do.

★ Failure is not the worst thing in the world. The very worst is not to try.

★ Faith without work is like an automobile without gas.

★ The fellow who's always leaning on his family tree never seems to get out of the woods.

★ The one thing worse than a quitter is the man who is afraid to start.

★ Promises may get friends, but it is performance that keeps them.

★ We make our future by the best use of the present.

★ People who live by the Golden Rule today never have to apologise for their actions tomorrow.

★ Unexpressed ideas are of no more value than kernels in a nut before it has been cracked.

★ Some people entertain ideas; others put them to work.

★ Good intentions die unless they are executed.

★ Leisure is a beautiful garment, but it will not do for constant wear.

★ It isn't how high you go in life that counts, but how you got there.

★ Works, not words, are the proof of love.

★ Even when opportunity knocks, a man still has to get off his seat and open the door.

★ For success, try aspiration, inspiration, and perspiration.

★ If you itch for success, keep on scratching.

★ A spoken word and a thrown stone cannot be recalled.

★ You can't clean up this old world with soft soap; it takes grit.

★ The world we live in is old-fashioned. It still judges a man by what he does.

Adolescence

★ Adolescence is when children start bringing up their parents.

* Adolescence is the awkward age when a child is too old to say something cute and too bound to say something sensible.
* Adolescence is something like a hitch in the army —you'd hate to have missed it, but you'd hate to repeat it.
* An adolescent is a youth old enough to dress himself if he could just remember where he dropped his clothes.
* Adolescence is the period when children are certain they will never be as stupid as their parents.
* An adolescent is a minor who is sometimes a major problem.
* Adolescence is a period of rapid change. Between the ages of twelve and seventeen, for example, a child may see his parents age twenty years.

Adversity

* Adversity is the only diet that will reduce a fat head.
* We learn some things from prosperity, but we learn many more from adversity.
* He who swells in prosperity will shrink in adversity.
* Adversity is never pleasant, but sometimes it's possible to learn lessons from it that can be learned in no other way.
* Another thing learned in adversity is that a tyre isn't the only thing you can patch.
* When things get rough, remember : It's the rubbing that brings out the shine.
* Your character is what you have left when you've lost everything you can lose.
* The address of character is often carved on the corner of Adversity Avenue and Determination Drive.
* Character, like sweet herbs, should give off its finest fragrance when pressed.
* The difficulties of life are intended to make us better — not bitter.
* There are two ways of meeting difficulties: alter the difficulties, or alter yourself to meet them.
* The friends you make in prosperity are those you lose in adversity.
* A real friend will tell you your faults and follies in times of prosperity, and assist you with his hand and heart in times of adversity.

★ Prosperity makes friends; adversity tries them.

★ The ladder of life is full of splinters, but you never realise it until you begin to slide down.

★ Love is a fabric which never fades, no matter how often it is washed in the water of adversity and grief.

Advertising

★ Sign in a florist's window: "Smoking, or forgetting your wife's birthday, can be hazardous to your health."

★ Where we go and what we do advertises what we are.

★ Advertising can be very expensive, especially if your wife can read.

★ In good times businessmen want to advertise; in bad times they have to.

★ Where we go and what we do advertises what we are.

★ Advertising helps raise the standard of living by raising the standard of longing.

★ Advertising is what transforms a yawn into a yearn.

★ Anti-cigarette commercial: "Truth or cancer-quences.

★ Advertising is what tells us which luxuries we can't do without.

Advice

★ Advice is like mushrooms. The wrong kind can prove fatal.

★ Never give advice before you're asked — or after!

★ Advice is least heeded when most needed.

★ Successful men follow the same advice they prescribe for others.

★ To profit from good advice requires more wisdom than to give it.

★ Some people never take advice from anybody; others take advice from everybody.

★ Advice is like a laxative — easy to take but hard to predict the outcome.

★ Advice to some people: If you had your life to live over — don't do it!

★ Advice is like snow — the softer it falls, the deeper it goes.

★ Never give advice — sell it!

★ Advice to men over fifty: Keep an open mind and a closed refrigerator.

★ Advice is like medicine — the correct dosage works wonders, but an overdose can be dangerous.

★ Advice is the one thing which is "more blessed to give than to receive."

★ The better the advice, the harder it is to take.

★ Advice is which the wise don't need and fools won't take.

★ When a man gets too old to set a bad example, he usually starts giving good advice.

★ The only time to give advice is when it is asked for — and then only in small doses.

★ People sensible enough to give good advice are also sensible enough not to.

★ A pint of example is worth a gallon of advice.

★ The best way to lose a friend is to tell him something for his own good.

★ The best thing one friend can do for another is to refrain from giving advice.

★ A juvenile delinquent usually prefers vice to advice.

★ The worst thing about growing old is having to listen to a lot of advice from one's children.

★ Old age is that period when a man is too old to take advice but young enough to give it.

★ Three cases where supply exceeds demand are: taxes, trouble, and advice.

★ Free advice is often overpriced.

Age

★ Age is what makes furniture worth more and people worth less.

★ Which do you suppose ages faster — whiskey or the man who drinks it?

★ Age is like love. It cannot be hidden.

★ Forty is the age when you begin to realise how much fun you had when you were twenty.

★ Old age is an island surrounded by death.

★ The older the fiddle, the sweeter the tune.

★ The oldest trees often bear the sweetest fruit.

★ Age is like love: it cannot be hid.

★ Age imprints more wrinkles in the mind than it does on the face.

★ By the time a man finds greener pastures, he's too old to climb the fence.

★ Age is the best possible fire extinguisher for flaming youth.

★ Sixty-five is the age when one acquires sufficient experience to lose his job.

★ Age has nothing to do with learning new ways to be stupid.

★ Hardening of the heart ages people more quickly than hardening of the arteries.

★ Twenty-nine is a wonderful age for a man to be — and for a woman to stay.

★ The dangerous age is any time between one and ninety-nine.

★ Age stiffens the joints and thickens some brains.

★ Many of us are at the "metallic age" — gold in our teeth, silver in our hair, and lead in our pants.

★ Age doesn't always bring wisdom. Sometimes age comes alone.

★ Life not only begins at forty — it begins to show.

★ Youth looks ahead, old age looks back, and middle age looks tired.

★ It's a sign of age if you feel like the morning after the night before, and you haven't been anywhere.

★ The three ages of man are youth, middle age and, "My, but you are looking well."

★ In this life the old believe everything, the middle-aged suspect everything, and the young know everything.

★ Everybody wants to live a long time, but nobody wants to get old.

★ It's so sad that people are like plants — some go to seed with age and others go to pot.

★ Some people grow up and spread cheer; others just grow up and spread.

Alarm Clocks

★ One thing an alarm clock never rouses is our better nature.

★ There's a new alarm clock on the market for actors. It doesn't ring-it applauds.

★ The trouble with alarm clocks is that they always go off when you're asleep.

★ An alarm clock is a device that makes men rise and whine.

Alcoholics

★ The favourite drink of an alcoholic is the next one.

★ To escape alcoholism is simple. Never take the drink just before the second one.

★ An alcoholic can neither live with alcohol nor without it.

★ An alcoholic is not one who drinks too much, but one who can't drink enough.

★ Alcohol is like love: the first kiss is magic, the second is intimate, the third is routine. And after that you just take the girl's clothes off.

★ Young men are apt to think themselves wise enough, as drunken are apt to think themselves sober enough.

★ The favourite drink of an alcoholic is the next one.

★ Some folks drink liquor as if they want to be mentioned in "BOOZE WHO."

Ambition

★ We rate ability in men by what they finish, not by what they attempt.

★ Some fellows dream of worthy accomplishments, while others stay awake and do them.

★ Every accomplishment, great or small, starts with the right decision, "I'll Try."

★ Don't just stand there — do something!

★ Don't sit back and take what comes. Go after what you want.

★ The fellow who has an abundance of push gets along very well without pull.

★ Watch out for ambition! It can get you into a lot of hard work.

★ A man with a burning ambition is seldom fired.

★ The ambition of some girls is to make a man a good husband.

★ Ambition without determination has no destination.

★ There are only two kinds of failures; the man who will do nothing he is told, and the man who will do nothing else.

★ Abraham Lincoln was great, not because he once lived in a cabin, but because he got out of it.

★ Don't wait for your ship to come in if you haven't sent one out.

★ The man with PUSH will pass the man with PULL.

★ The best ammunition to fight poverty is a load of ambition fired with effort towards a definite goal.

Ancestors

★ You can't choose your ancestors, but that's fair enough. They probably wouldn't have chosen you.

★ The man who has nothing to boast but his ancestors is like a potato — the only good belonging to him is underground.

★ The man who boasts only if his roots is conceding that he belongs to a family that's better dead than alive.

★ The measure of a man's character is not what he gets from his ancestors, but what he leaves his descendants.

Anger

★ "Anger" is just one letter short of danger.

★ Anger is a wind that blows out the lamp of the mind.

★ He is a fool who cannot get angry, but he is a wise man who will not.

* Hot words never resulted in cool judgement.
* He who has a sharp tongue soon cuts his own throat.
* Speak when you are angry and you will make the best speech you will ever regret.
* An angry man is seldom reasonable; a reasonable man is seldom angry.
* Anger is a state that starts with madness and ends with regret.
* When angry count ten before speaking.
* For every minute you're angry, you lose sixty seconds of happiness.
* Men with clenched fists cannot shake hands.
* No one can be reasonable and angry at the same time.
* The world needs more warm hearts and fewer hot heads.
* Anyone who angers you conquers you.
* The emptier the pot, the quicker the boil — watch your temper!
* Anger makes your mouth work faster than your mind.
* Form the habit of closing your mouth firmly when angry.
* The greatest remedy for anger is delay.

Appearance

* Life not only begins at forty — it begins to show.
* A long face and a broad mind are rarely found under the same hat.
* A father is usually more pleased to have his child look like him than act like him.
* Any girl can be glamorous. All she has to do is stand still and look stupid.
* The Lord gives us our faces, but we must provide the expression.
* The surest sign that a man is not great is when he strives to look great.
* Don't judge a man by the clothes he wears. God made one; the tailor, the other.
* A plastic surgeon increases your face value.

★ People seldom notice old clothes if you wear a big smile.

★ Few women believe what their mirrors and bathroom scales tell them.

★ The real secret of looking young is being young.

Appreciation

★ You must speak to be heard, but sometimes you have to shut up to be appreciated.

★ Appreciate what you have before what you haven't.

★ The best way to appreciate your job is to imagine yourself without it.

★ Don't forget that appreciation is always appreciated.

★ Appreciation is like an insurance policy. It has to be renewed occasionally.

★ The world's most unsatisfied hunger is the hunger for appreciation.

★ A slap on the back often pushes out the chest.

★ A single rose for living is better than a costly wreath at the grave.

★ Carve your name on hearts-not on marble.

Argument

★ The only people who really listen to an argument are the neighbours.

★ Many an argument is sound- and only sound!

★ The more arguments you win, the fewer friends you'll have.

★ The weaker the argument, the stronger the words.

★ The best way to get the best of an argument is to listen to it at a safe distance.

★ An argument produces plenty of heat, but not much light.

★ In an argument, the best weapon to hold is your tongue.

★ An argument is where two people are trying to get in the last word first.

★ People who know the least always argue the most.

★ An argument is a collision in which two trains of thought are derailed.

★ One thing a man learns from an argument with a woman is how to be a good loser.

★ An argument is a question with two sides—and no end.

★ Don't argue at the dinner table. The one who is not hungry always wins the argument.

★ When an argument flares up, the wise man quenches it with silence.

★ Never argue with your wife for it is as useless as trying to blow out a lightbulb.

★ Many a family argument has been saved by the doorbell or telephone.

★ An argument is like a country road; you never know where it'll lead.

★ An ounce of facts is worth a ton of arguments.

★ Arguing about religion is much easier than practicing it.

Attention

★ The only thing some people pay is attention.

★ A good listener is one who can give you his full attention without hearing a word you say.

★ The easiest way to get a kid's attention is to stand in front of the TV set.

★ Pay attention to what a man is, not what he has been.

★ The quickest way to get a lot of individual attention is to make a big mistake.

★ Troubles and weeds thrive on lack of attention.

★ When a child pays attention to his parents, they're probably whispering.

Authority

★ Nothing intoxicates some people like a sip of authority.

★ Authority is like a bank account. The more you draw on it, the less you have.

★ Give authority to some people and they grow; give it to others and they swell.

B

Bachelors

★ It may be that bachelors make more mistake than married men—but they don't make the big one.

★ A bachelor usually wants one single thing in life — himself!

★ A bachelor is a guy who leans towards women, but not far enough to lose his balance.

★ To the bachelor, horror films are pictures of a wedding.

★ Bachelors, like detergents, work fast and leave no rings.

★ A bachelor is a rolling stone that gathers no moss.

★ A bachelor never gets over the idea that he is a thing of beauty and boy forever.

★ A bachelor may have no buttons on his shirt, but a married man often has no shirt.

★ Bachelors avoid a woman who has a ring in her voice.

★ A bachelor is a man who takes advantage of the fact that marriage isn't compulsory.

Banks

★ Bank interest on a loan is so high that if you can afford to pay it you don't need the loan.

★ A bank is a financial institution where you can borrow money if you can present sufficient evidence to show that you don't need it.

★ Many people seem to think a home is only good to borrow money on.

★ Modern prosperity means two cars in the garage, a boat in the drive way, and a note due at the bank.

Bargains

★ Nowadays everything is a bargain — because by the time you get it home the price has gone up.

★ A bargain is when two people are sure they got the better of each other.

★ A bargain is something that looks better than it is and sells for less than it was.

✶ There would be fewer divorces if women hunted for husbands with as much thought as they hunt for bargains.

✶ The best exercise today is hunting for bargains.

✶ Heaven is a bargain, however great the cost.

✶ One of the problems of modern life is for a husband to teach his wife that every bargain costs money.

✶ Don't buy it for a song — unless you're sure you know what the pitch is.

Bigamy

✶ The penalty for bigamy is two mothers-in-law.

✶ A bigamist is a chap who has had one too many.

✶ Bigamy is having one wife too many — monogamy is often the same.

✶ Bigamy is the only crime on the books where two rites make a wrong.

✶ Most men would like to have a wife who's beautiful, understanding, economical, and a good cook. Unfortunately, the law allows a man only one wife!

Books

✶ The Bible is not only the world's best seller, it is man's best purchase.

✶ How-to-get-rich books are now filed under FICTION.

✶ The one book that always has a sad ending is a cheque book.

✶ Sign in a South Dakota bookstore, "Read a good novel before Hollywood ruins it."

✶ The trouble with speed reading is that by the time you realise a book is boring, you've finished reading it.

✶ In a library the books that aren't dirty are the ones that are dusty.

✶ A poor appetite for good books eventually leads to intellectual malnutrition.

✶ So many books are now being written on how to speak that there ought to be a market for one on how to shut up.

✶ Some books you can't put down, and others you dare not put down when there are children in the house.

★ The only book that really tells you where you can go on your vacation is your cheque book.

★ A classic is a book which people praise highly but never read.

★ Generally, women don't like the dictionary, because it has the first and the last word.

★ To the average girl the most helpful books are mother's cookbook and father's cheque book.

★ In today's novels the boy always gets the girls — at least once in every chapter.

★ A lot of modern novels have one common failure — their covers are too far apart.

★ Novels are like wives; you don't talk about them. But movies are different; they're like mistresses, and you can brag a bit.

Bosses

★ Before you have an argument with your boss, you'd better take a good look at both sides — his side and the outside.

★ The only time it's safe to tell the boss where to get off is when he falls asleep on the bus.

★ The hardest job in the world is telling the boss the computer proved him wrong.

★ A certain boss when asked how many people work for him replied, "About half of them."

★ Some bosses take great pains — and give them to others.

★ Be loyal to your boss because the next one might be worse.

★ A man's best boss is a well-trained conscience.

★ The fellow who is fired with enthusiasm for his work is seldom fired by his boss.

Brains

★ Age stiffens the joints and thickens some brains.

★ There's no tax on brains; the take would be too small.

★ Be sure your brain is engaged before putting your mouth in gear.

★ Always remember that a man is not rewarded for having brains, but for using them.

★ The human brain is the apparatus with which we think we think.

★ If there is a substitute for brains it has to be silence.

★ Brains and beauty are nature's gifts; character is your own achievement.

★ Keeping clean between the ears may be more important than keeping clean behind the ears.

★ Nature abhors a vacuum. When a head lacks brains, nature fills it with conceit.

★ There are more idle brains than idle hands.

★ There is no real substitute for brains, but silence does pretty well.

★ The human tongue is only a few inches from the brain, but when you listen to some people talk, they seem miles apart.

Budgets

★ There's nothing tighter than next year's budget and this year's bikini.

★ A budget enables you to spend money without enjoying it.

★ Balancing the budget is when money in the bank and the days of the month come out together.

★ The trouble with a budget is that it won't budge.

★ A budget is an orderly way of discovering that you can't live on what you're earning.

★ A budget is an attempt to live below your yearnings.

★ A budget is what you stay within if you go without.

★ A balanced budget is when the month and the money run out together.

★ We could get along better with fewer economists and more economisers.

Bureaucracy

★ In a bureaucracy, they shoot the bull, pass the buck, and make seven copies of everything.

★ The proper way to greet a visiting bureaucrat is to rule out the red tape.

★ Bureaucracy is based on a willingness to either pass the buck or spend it.

★ What's needed in government is more horse sense and less nonsense.

Business

★ A man's accomplishment in business depends partly on whether he keeps his mind or his feet on the desk.

★ Doing business without advertising is like winking at a girl in the dark. You know what you're doing, but she doesn't.

★ Never give advice — sell it!

★ If you want to go far in business, you'll have to stay close to it.

★ In the business world transactions speak louder than words.

★ Competition may be the life of trade, but it's often the death of profit.

★ A scissor sharpener is the only person whose business is good when things are dull.

★ Business is like a wheelbarrow — it stands still unless somebody pushes it.

★ The business to stay out of is the other fellow's.

★ A good business manager hires optimists as salesmen and pessimists to run the credit department.

★ Business is like a bicycle — when it isn't moving forward at a good speed it wobbles.

★ Business will continue to go where invited and will remain where appreciated.

★ A shady business never produces a sunny life.

★ Business is made good by yearning, learning, and earning.

★ Business is a lot like tennis — those who don't serve well wind up losing.

★ He who has the habit of smiling at the cash register instead of the customer won't be smiling long.

★ One trouble with credit business is that there is too much stall in instalments.

★ Business is like an automobile. It won't run itself, except downhill.

★ Business is tough these days. If a man does something wrong he gets fined; if he does something right he gets taxed.

* Humour is the lubricating oil of business. It prevents friction and wins good will.
* No business opportunity is ever lost. If you fumble your competitor will find it.
* The man who lives only for himself runs a very small business.

C

Careful driving

* Drive towards others as you would have others drive towards you.
* To drive carefully — just drive like everybody else is crazy.
* Glasses can make driving a lot safer. Providing, of course, they're worn instead of emptied.
* By driving carefully you can help preserve two of our most valuable resources — gasoline and you.
* Sign on a florist truck, "Drive carefully. The next load may be yours."
* A good safety slogan : "Drive scared."
* Driving is a lot like baseball — it's the number of times you get home safely that counts.
* Drive carefully! The life you save could be someone who owes you money.
* Better be patient on the road than a patient in the hospital.
* The careful driver stops at a railroad crossing for a minute; the careless one, forever.
* You should drive your car as if your family was in the other car.
* Always drive so that your licence will expire before you do.
* When driving near schools, open your eyes and save the pupils.
* Drive with care. Life has no spare.
* Brains and brakes prevent pains and aches.
* The best way to stay alive on the highway is to limit the speed — not speed the limit.

★ Don't drive as if you owned the road — drive as if you owned the car.
★ If you drive carefully you avoid the "mourning after."
★ Advice to motorists: If you want to stay in the pink, watch the red and the green.
★ The best rule in driving through five o'clock traffic is to try and avoid being a part of the six o'clock news.

Change

★ Some people continue to change jobs, mates, and friends — but never think of changing themselves.
★ Constant change is here to stay.
★ Many people hate any change that doesn't jingle in their pockets.
★ New ideas hurt some minds the same as new shoes hurt some feet.
★ Change is what a person wants on a vacation — and a lot of currency too.

Children

★ Adolescence is when children start bringing up their parents.
★ Life's golden age is when the children are too old to need baby sitters and too young to borrow the family car.
★ An alarm clock is a device for awakening people who don't have small children.
★ Children love to break things — especially rules.
★ Children are like wet cement. Whatever falls on them makes an impression.
★ The only thing that children wear out faster than shoes are parents and teachers.
★ Children disgrace us in public by behaving just like we do at home.
★ The best time to put the children to bed is when you can.
★ Children are very much like airplanes; you hear only of the ones that crash.
★ If you are disgusted and upset with your children, just imagine how God must feel about His!
★ It's real nice for children to have pets until the pets start having children.

★ Children are unpredictable. You never know when they're going to catch you in a lie.

★ Childhood is that wonderful period when all you need to do to lose weight is take a bath.

★ Children need strength to lean on, a shoulder to cry on, and an example to learn from.

★ Rearing children is the biggest "heir-conditioning" job ever undertaken.

★ When a child listens to his mother, he's probably on the telephone extension.

★ Modern parents think children should be seen, not heard; children think parents should be neither seen nor heard.

★ The best thing to spend on children is your time.

★ Any child who gets raised strictly by the book is probably a first edition.

★ Almost every child would learn to write sooner if allowed to do homework on wet cement.

★ Most children seldom misquote you; they repeat what you shouldn't have said word for word.

★ Among the best home furnishings are children.

★ Cleanliness may be next to godliness, but in childhood it's next to impossible.

★ Sending your child to college is like sending your clothes to the laundry. You get what you put in, but sometimes you can hardly recognise it.

★ Every father should remember that one day his son will follow his example instead of his advice.

★ We learn from experience. A man never wakes up his second baby just to see it smile.

★ As the gardener is responsible for the products of his garden, so the family is responsible for the character and conduct of its children.

★ Playing golf is like raising children — you keep thinking you'll do better next time.

★ The best possible infant care is to keep one end full and the other end dry.

★ A real family man is one who looks at his new child as an addition rather than a deduction.

★ Children often hold a marriage together by keeping their parents so busy they don't have time to quarrel.

★ When it comes to music lessons, most kids make it a practice not to practice.

★ People who say they sleep like a baby haven't got one.

★ There's only one perfect child in the world and every mother has it.

★ Child psychology is what children manage their parents with.

★ The hardest people to convince that they're ready to retire are children at bedtime.

★ Sleep is something that science cannot abolish — but babies can.

★ Nothing improves a television program as much as getting the children to bed.

Chivalry

★ Chilvalry is a man's inclination to defend a woman against every man but himself.

★ Chivalry is what a husband displays towards somebody else's wife.

★ In the "good old days" men stood up for women — but there were no buses then.

★ Chivalry is when a man picks up a girl's handkerchief, even if she's not pretty.

★ Chivalry is opening the door and standing aside so some female can rush in and get the job you're after.

Choice

★ Few people make a deliberate choice between good and evil; the choice is between what we want to do and what we ought to do.

★ It is much wiser to choose what you say than to say what you choose.

★ A conference is a meeting to decide when and where the next meeting will be held.

★ A conference is nothing more than an organised way of postponing a decision.

★ Always take plenty of time to make a snap decision.

★ If you're going to pull decisions out of a hat, be sure you're wearing the right hat.

★ Many a woman's final decision is not the last one she makes.

★ If fate hands you a lemon, try to make lemonade.

★ Nature gives man corn, but man must grind it; God gives man a will, but man must make the right choices.

★ In most marriages the husband is the provider and the wife is the decider.

Cigarettes

★ It takes most men about two years to completely quit smoking cigarettes and twice as long to quit bragging about it.

★ When everything else fails as a cure for smoking cigarettes, try carrying wet matches.

★ The best way to stop smoking cigarettes is to marry a woman who objects to it.

★ Some people feel that a cigarette is not harmful if they borrow it from somebody else.

★ Just about us many people will quit smoking cigarettes this week as last week — and a lot of them will be the same people.

★ If you don't think smoking cigarettes makes a woman's voice harsh, try dropping cigarette ashes on her rug.

★ Cigarettes are killers that travel in packs.

★ A new cigarette offers coupons good for a cemetery lot.

★ A person pays twice for his cigarettes. Once when he gets them and, second, when they get him.

★ Walking a mile for a cigarette may be healthier than smoking one.

★ Anti-cigarette commercial: "Truth or cancerquences."

★ Sign in Boston hospital: "We don't sell cigarettes — we love you too much."

★ Self-control is giving up smoking cigarettes; extreme self-control is not telling anybody about it.

★ One of the nice things about smoking a pipe is that you can't light the wrong end.

Common sense

★ The biggest shortage of all is the shortage of common sense.

★ Common sense is the knack of seeing things as they are, and doing things as they ought to be done.

★ It seems that common sense isn't as common as it used to be.

★ An unusual amount of common sense is sometimes called wisdom.

★ Most people have good common sense, but they use it only in an emergency.

★ It is a thousand times better to have common sense without an education than to have an education without common sense.

★ Common sense is something you want the other fellow to show by accepting your ideas and conclusions.

★ Emotions make the world go round, but common sense keeps it from going too fast.

★ Common sense is the sixth sense, given to us by the Creator to keep the other five from making fools of themselves — and us.

★ It's unfortunate that common sense isn't more common.

★ Common sense is genius dressed in its working clothes.

★ It is extremely embrassing to come to your senses and find out you haven't any.

★ Horse sense means stable thinking.

★ Love quickens all the senses — except common sense.

★ Philosophy is nothing but common sense in a dress suit.

★ Psychiatry is just common sense clothed in a language no one can understand.

★ Science is nothing but trained and organised common sense.

★ Wisdom is nothing more than common sense refined by learning and experience.

★ The door to wisdom swings on hinges of common sense and uncommon thoughts.

Communism

★ The difference between communism and democracy is — plenty!

Communists

★ A Communist is a Socialist in a hurry.

Compliments

★ Don't forget that appreciation is always appreciated.

★ It's easy to keep from being a bore. Just praise the person to whom you're talking.

★ The best way to compliment your wife is frequently.

★ A compliment a day keeps divorce far, far away.

★ It's ironic but the toughest thing to take gracefully is a compliment.

★ A compliment is the soft soap that wipes out a dirty look.

★ Compliments are like perfume: to be inhaled, not swallowed.

★ A hammer sometimes misses its mark — a bouquet, never.

★ There's a difference between paying compliments and paying for them.

★ Nobody has ever been bored by someone paying them a compliment.

Computers

★ The hardest job in the world is in telling the boss the computer proved him wrong.

★ The computer is a great invention. There are as many mistakes as ever, but now they're nobody's fault.

★ Computers are like Men...

★ ...In order to get their attention, you have to turn them on.

★ ...They are supposed to help solve problems, but half the time they are the problem

★ ... they have a lot of data, but are still clueless.

★ ... They are what you say, but not what you mean.

★ Computers are like Women...

★ ... No one but the Creator understands their internal logic.

★ ... Even your smallest mistakes are stored in long-term memory for later retrieval.

★ ...You do the same thing for years, and suddenly it's wrong.

★ There is now a female computer on the market. You don't ask it anything, but it tells you anyway.

★ Computers will never replace human beings entirely. Someone has to complain about the errors.

★ Some computers are almost human. When they make a mistake they put the blame on another computer.

★ To err is human. But to really louse it up, it takes a computer.

★ A girl said to her boyfriend, "Remember, I'm a computer date, and I don't want to be bent, folded, or spindled."

Confidence

★ You must first be a believer if you would be an achiever.

★ The line between self-confidence and conceit is very narrow.

★ Confidence is the feeling you have before you fully understand the situation.

★ There are two reasons why we don't trust people; one, because we don't know them; and the other, because we do.

★ Belief in God will help you most if you also believe in yourself.

Conscience

★ To know what is right and not do it is as bad as doing wrong.

★ A budget is like a conscience — it doesn't keep you from spending, but it makes you feel guilty about it.

★ Conscience keeps more people awake than coffee.

★ Conscience is like a baby. It has to go to sleep before you can.

★ Conscience is what hurts when everything else feels good.

★ No one works his conscience so hard that it needs a vacation.

★ The line is often too busy when conscience wishes to speak.

★ Conscience, like a pencil, needs to be sharpened occasionally.

★ When you have a fight with your conscience and get licked, you win.

★ The best tranquiliser, is a good conscience.

★ A gash in the conscience may disfigure the soul.

★ A fellow's conscience works best while he's being watched.

★ Conscience is not the voice of God; it is the gift of God.

★ As long as your conscience is your friend, never mind about your enemies.

★ Nothing goes to sleep as easy as one's conscience.

★ Conscience is the only mirror that doesn't flatter.

★ Conscience is something inside that bothers you when nothing outside does.

★ The world is composed of the takers and the givers. The takers may eat better, but the givers sleep better.

★ Ignorance is an opiate that lulls a conscience to sleep.

★ What the world needs is an amplifier for the still, small voice.

★ God may forgive your sin, but your nervous system won't.

Cost of living

★ It seems the only thing that hasn't increased in cost is free advice.

★ Airplane fares have been increased considerably. Even the cost of going up is going up.

★ Anybody who thinks the automobile has made people lazy never had to pay for one.

★ Today's cars keep a person strapped without safetybelts.

★ A good way to make your present car run better is to have a salesman quote you the price of a new one.

★ The new cars give you more room by removing the bulge in you wallet.

★ Bank interest on a loan is so high that if you can afford to pay it you don't need the loan.

★ It now costs more to amuse a child than it once did to educate his father.

★ Christmas is the time of the year when Santa Claus comes down the chimney and your savings go down the drain.

★ Christmas is a time when a lot of others besides Santa find themselves in the red.

★ A man complains about the food when he eats at home and about the price when he eats out.

★ When someone complains about prices today, one thing is certain — he's buying, not selling.

★ The way things are now you're lucky if you can make one end meet.

★ The only way to beat the high cost of living is to stop living.

★ They call it a "dream house" because it usually costs twice as much as you dreamed it would.

★ Beware of the high cost of low living.

★ It's easy to make money these days — it's only hard to make a living.

★ Whatever the cost of living is, it's worth it.

★ Descending prices, like falling stars, always seem to fall in some other place.

★ The cost of living is the only thing that defies the law of gravitation; it keeps going up without ever coming down.

★ Have you ever noticed that the things you never wanted are considerably cheaper?

★ There's no better diet than eating only what you can afford.

★ A gardener raises a few things, a farmer raises many things, and the middleman raises everything.

★ If food prices go any higher, toothpicks may become a status symbol.

★ If a hen knew the current price of eggs, she wouldn't cackle — she'd crow!

★ These days there are two kinds of people cutting down on food — those who can't afford the calories, and those who can't afford the prices.

★ In meat markets the meat may be tender, but the price is tough.

★ Nothing makes food less fattening than being too expensive.

★ At today's food prices, the man who goes bankrupt can blame it on what he ate.

★ It's not the coffee that keeps folks awake these days, but the price of it.

★ The way food prices are going up, more people are being put on diets by their accountants than by their doctors.

★ Inflated food prices are hard to swallow.

★ Food prices are so high that it's no longer possible to bite off more than you can chew.

★ Nothing is dirt cheap any more, except gossip.

★ The way the cost of living and taxes are today, you might as well marry for love.

* Nothing is as dead as yesterday's news — except yesterday's prices.
* The only time where ends meet nowadays is on a football field.
* The only walk more expensive than a walk down a church aisle is a walk down a supermarket aisle.
* Supermarkets are like churches. People walk down the aisles saying, "Lord, help us."
* Supermarkets are very convenient. They permit a shopper to go broke in one store.
* A supermarket used to be a place where people came out with a bundle. Now it's where they go in with a bundle — of money!

Courtship

* More and more lovely courtships sail into the sea of matrimony, and finally sink into the rocky storms of divorce.
* Courtship is that period during which the female decides whether or not she can do any better.
* Courtship, unlike proper punctuation, is a period before a sentence.
* Courtship is the part of a girl's life which comes between the lipstick and the broomstick.
* Divorce records show that many married couples spend too much time in court and not enough time courting.
* Platonic friendship is the name given to the period between the first look and the first kiss.
* The fellow who once enjoyed chasing girls now has a son who can't find any who will run.
* Today young people start going steady with the opposite sex as soon as they learn there is one.

Cynics

* A cynic is a person who knows everything and believes nothing.
* Most cynics look both ways before crossing a one-way street.
* A cynic believes other people are as bad as he is.

★ An onion is the only thing that will make a cynic shed tears.

★ A pessimist expects nothing on a silver platter except tarnish.

D

Death

★ There are two places the jet planes have brought closer together — this world and the next.

★ Nothing improves a man's appearances as much as the photograph the newspapers use with his obituary.

★ On his examination paper a boy wrote, "A natural death is where you die by yourself without a doctor's help."

★ A new cigarette offers coupons good for a cemetery lot.

★ Nothing seems to make the cost of living as reasonable as pricing funerals.

★ The person who is never criticised is not breathing.

★ Death is not a period but a comma in the story of life.

★ People who are afraid of death are usually afraid of life.

★ Make this your motto: Don't die until you are dead.

★ No one is dead as long as he is remembered by someone.

★ When we die we leave behind us all that we have and take with us all that we are.

★ There are worse things than death for some people — take life, for instance.

★ Fame is chiefly a matter of dying at the right time.

★ A single rose for the living is better than a costly wreath at the grave.

★ In a world death is, we should have no time to hate.

★ Another difference between death and taxes is that death is frequently painless.

★ Death and taxes are inevitable, but death is not a repeater.

★ Perpetual worry will get you to one place ahead of time — the cemetery.

Debts

★ The man who borrows trouble is always in debt.

* Debt is what you get into if you spend as much as you tell your friends you earn.
* Running into debt is no trouble. Running into creditors is.
* The best possible thing to do with a debt is pay it.
* If you listen to the loan company commercials, you'll almost believe you can borrow yourself out of debt.
* Some people use one half of their ingenuity to get into debt and the other half to avoid paying it.
* Debt is like quicksand, and just about as hard to get out of.
* What you don't owe won't hurt you.
* Molehills of debt build mountains of worry.
* Some friends stick together until 'debt do them part.'
* Never forget a friend — especially if he owes you anything.
* Yesterday's luxuries are today's debts.
* Creditors have a better memory than debtors.
* About all you can do with money nowadays is owe it.
* Money may not make a person happy, but it keeps his creditors in a better frame of mind.
* As a general rule, prosperity is what keeps us in debt.
* A good salesman can talk you to debt.
* If you're not in style, the chances are you're out of debt.
* Blessed are the teenagers, for they shall inherit the national debt.
* Television sets are three dimensional. They give you height, width, and debt.
* The man who borrows trouble is always in debt.
* The only thing you can get without work is debt.

Diets

* Advice to men over fifty: Keep an open mind and a closed refrigerator.
* When you see a man wearing a baggy suit, either he has a great diet or a terrible tailor.
* You can't reduce by talking about it. You must keep your mouth shut.
* Diets are so strict nowadays that the only thing dieters are allowed to have is hunger pains.
* There's no better diet than eating only what you can afford.

★ People who diet go to great lenghts to avoid great widths.
★ Dieting is the time when the days seem longer and the meals seem shorter.
★ A diet helps people gain weight slower.
★ Nowadays almost everybody is on a diet — due to high prices or high cholesterol.
★ Many people are on the new, "see-food" diet — you see food, but you don't eat it.
★ A diet is something you went off yesterday — or expect to start tomorrow.
★ A diet is what you keep putting off while you keep putting on.
★ Diet tip: To indulge is to bulge.
★ A diet is something that will take the starch out of you.
★ Some women diet to keep their girlish figure; others, keep their boyish husbands.
★ The best way to lose weight is to eat all you want of everything you don't like.
★ The ideal diet is expressed in four words: "No more, thank you."
★ Destiny shapes our ends, but calorie intake is what shapes our middle.
★ A diet is the only thing that shows a gain by showing a loss.
★ A diet is like a ball game. You're the umpire behind the "home plate."
★ The best exercise is to exercise discretion at the dining table.
★ Just buying all those expensive diet foods can be very flattening.
★ To feel "fit as a fiddle" you must tone down your middle.
★ A great invention for dieters would be a refrigerator that weighs you every time you open the door.

Doubt

★ When in doubt, tell the truth.
★ Never put a question mark where God has put a period.
★ Some folks demand the benefit of the doubt when there isn't any.
★ When in doubt, don't.
★ Doubt makes the mountain which faith can move.

★ Many people believe their doubts and doubt their beliefs.
★ Think of doubt as an invitation to think.
★ Feed your faith and your doubts will starve to death.
★ No one can live in doubt when he has prayed in faith.

Dreams

★ Castles in the air all right until you try to move into them.
★ Some people dream in technicolour — others add sound effects.
★ Don't be unhappy if your dreams never come true — just be thankful your nightmares don't.
★ Some men believe in dreams until they marry one.
★ We cannot dream ourselves into what we could be.
★ If you want your dreams to come true, don't oversleep.
★ No dream comes true until you wake up and go to work.
★ A house is made of walls and beams; a home is built with love and dreams.
★ Between tomorrow's dream and yesterday's regret is today's opportunity.
★ Those who think they are dreamers are usually just sleepers.
★ Day dreams at the steering wheel lead to nightmares in the hospital.

Drunkards

★ A drunkard can live neither with alcohol nor without it.
★ There's nothing more stubborn than a drunkard trying to convince you he isn't.
★ A drunkard can't make both ends meet because he's too busy making one end drink.
★ Some folks drink liquor as if they want to be mentioned in "BOOZE WHO."
★ Warning: Boozers are losers.
★ It's when a man gets tight as a drum that he makes the most noise.

Drunken driving

★ Cars and bars mean stars and scars.

* It's better to sit tight than to attempt to drive tight.
* If you drink like a fish, swim—don't drive.
* The hand that lifts the cup that cheers, should not be used to shift the gears.
* Watch out for Sunday drivers who started out Saturday night.
* Traffic warning sign: "Heads you win—cocktails you lose."
* There is only one way to drink and drive—hazardously!

Duty

* The value of the Bible doesn't consist in merely knowing it, but in obeying it.
* Generally speaking, duty is what we expect of others.
* God never imposes a duty without giving time and strength to perform it.
* The best way to get rid of your duties is to discharge them.
* Duty makes us do things well, but love makes us do them beautifully.
* A reformer sees his duty and overdoes it.

E

Economists

* The easiest way to start an argument these days is to get two economists together.
* An economist is a man who figures out tomorrow why the things he predicted yesterday didn't happen today.
* We could get along better with fewer economists and more economisers.
* An economist usually has a plan to do something with somebody else's money.
* Economists now say we move in cycles instead of running in circles. It may sound better, but it means the same thing.
* An economist can tell you what to do with your money after you've done something else with it.

★ An economist recently completed writing a book titled *The Short Story of Money*. The book contains only seven words, "Here it is and there it goes."

Education

★ Teaching children to count is not as important as teaching them what counts.

★ Education is a funny thing. At eighteen we knew all the answers — forty years later even the questions confuse us.

★ Among the few things more expensive than an education these days is the lack of it.

★ Some folks are so highly educated they can bore you on any subject.

★ Don't call it education unless it has taught you life's true values.

★ A person isn't educated unless he has learned how little he already knows.

★ If you think getting an education is expensive, try not getting one.

★ Education enables a person to get into more intelligent trouble.

★ Education is what you get from reading the small print in a contract. Experience is what you get from not reading it.

★ You can buy education, but wisdom is a gift from God.

★ An educated person is one who knows a great deal and says little about it.

★ Education pays less when you are an educator.

★ The chief benefit of education is to discover how little we know.

★ Education should include knowledge of what to do with it.

★ An educated man will sit up all night and worry over things a fool never dreamed of.

★ Education is not received. It is *achieved*.

★ No man is fully educated until he learns to read himself.

★ It's what we learn after we know it all that really counts.

★ The true object of education should be to train one to think clearly and act rightly.

★ Education is not a head full of facts, but knowing how and where to find facts.

★ It's not what is poured into a student that counts, but what is planted.
★ Education is an ornament in prosperity and a refuge in adversity.
★ Education means developing the mind, not stuffing the memory.
★ Experience has been described as "Compulsory Education."
★ A little learning may be a dangerous thing — but it's still safer than total ignorance.
★ Some students drink at the fountain of knowledge. Other just gargle.
★ Only hungry minds can become educated.
★ School and education should not be confused; it is only school that can be made easy.

Encouragement

★ A slap on the back often pushes out the chest.
★ A slap on the back doesn't always mean encouragement — mosquitoes get it too!
★ Pat others on the back, not yourself.
★ The best thing to do behind a person's back is pat it.
★ Don't forget that a pat on the back can cause a chin to go up and shoulders to go back.
★ Patting a fellow on the back is the best way to get a chip off his shoulder.

Enthusiasm

★ Enthusiasm is contagious — and so is the lack of it.
★ Enthusiasm is a good engine, but it needs intelligence for a driver.
★ There's always a good crop of food for thought. What we need is enough enthusiasm to harvest it.
★ Enthusiasm is apt to breed more action than accuracy.
★ The fellow who is fired with enthusiasm for his work is seldom fired by his boss.
★ Enthusiasm is the propelling force necessary for climbing the ladder of success.
★ Years wrinkle the skin, but lack of enthusiasm wrinkles the soul.
★ Genius is nothing more than inflamed enthusiasm.

Exaggeration

* When you make a mountain out of a molehill, don't expect anyone to climb up to see the view.
* One of the most difficult mountains for people to climb is the one they make out of a molehill.
* There are people so addicted to exaggeration that they can't tell the truth without lying.
* Exaggeration is a blood relative to falsehood, and almost as bad.
* Some folks never exaggerate. They just think big.
* Some people get all their mental exercise by climbing up and down molehills.
* Nothing makes a fish bigger than almost being caught.
* Gossip is like a balloon — it grows bigger with every puff.
* It isn't difficult to make a mountain out of a molehill — just add a little dirt.

Excuses

* If you have an excuse, don't use it.
* Most failures are expert at making excuses.
* Excuses fool no one but the person who makes them.
* A real man is one who finds excuses for others, but never for himself.
* Never give an excuse that you would not be willing to accept.
* When you don't want to do anything, one excuse is as good as another.
* The most unprofitable item ever manufactured is an excuse.
* Time wasted thinking up excuses would be better spent avoiding the need for them.

Executives

* When they say a man is a "born executive," they mean his father owns the business.
* A good executive is one who can make decisions quickly — and sometimes correctly.

★ Plaque on the desk of an executive: "Once I thought I was wrong — but I was mistaken."

★ An executive is a fellow who can take as long as he wants to make a snap decision.

★ Sign on an executive's desk: "Don't tell me what I mean. Let me figure it out myself."

★ If you want a job done fast, give it to a busy executive. He'll have his secretary do it.

★ An honest executive is one who shares the credit with the man who did all the work.

★ An executive is one who hires others to do the work he's supposed to do.

★ An executive is a man who talks to the visitors while others are doing the work.

Exercise

★ Jumping to conclusions is about the only exercise some people get.

★ Those who perform the modern dance exercise everything except discretion.

★ It's time to go on a diet when you notice you're puffing going down stairs.

★ Walking is good exercise if you can dodge those who aren't.

★ The exercise that wears most people out is running out of cash.

★ About the only exercise some young fellows get is running out of money and after women.

★ The best thing to get out of exercise is rest.

★ The only exercise some people get is pulling ice trays out of the refrigerator.

★ About the only part of the body that is over-exercised is the lower jaw.

★ The best exercise is to exercise discretion at the dining table.

★ If you must exercise, why not exercise kindness?

Experience

★ There is no sun without shadow, and it is essential to know the night.

☆ In the depth of winter one finally learns that within one there lay an invincible summer.

☆ We are all sculptors and painters, and our material is our own flesh and bones.

☆ If experience is the best teacher, many of us are mightily poor pupils.

☆ Experience has been described as "Compulsory Education."

☆ Experience is about the cheapest thing a fellow can get if he's smart enough to get it secondhand.

☆ Experience is what helps you make an old mistake in a new way.

☆ The wealth of experience is one possession that has not yet been taxed.

☆ About all some of us get from experience is experience.

☆ Experience is the best teacher, and considering what it costs, it should be.

☆ It requires experience to know how to use it.

☆ There is no way to get experience, except through experience.

☆ Experience makes a person better or bitter.

☆ Experience is like a comb- we generally get it when we turn bald.

☆ One may not reach the dawn save by the path of the night.

☆ Experience is not only an expensive teacher, but by the time you get through her school, life is over.

☆ Experience is often what you get when you were expecting something else.

☆ The school of experience would be more pleasant if there were a vacation once in a while.

☆ Experience is what you've got when you're too old to get a job.

☆ The school of experience never changes; it always issues its diplomas on the roughest grade of sandpaper.

☆ Experience is a form of knowledge acquired in only two ways — by doing and by being done.

☆ Experience is what makes your mistakes so familiar.

☆ Unused experience is a dead loss.

☆ Experience is one thing you can't get on the easy payment plan.

★ The proof that experience teaches us nothing is that the end of one love affair does not prevent us from beginning another.

★ Another reason why experience is the best teacher — she is always on the job.

★ Experience may be the best teacher, but she's not the prettiest.

★ The man who has to eat his own words never asks for another serving.

Experts

★ An expert can take something you already know and make it sound confusing.

★ An expert knows all the answers—if you ask the right questions.

★ The trouble with being an expert is that you can't turn to anybody else for advice.

★ An expert is always able to create confusion out of simplicity.

Extravagance

★ The remarkable thing about most of us is our ability to live beyond our means.

★ The average man's ambition is to be able to afford what he's spending.

★ Extravagance is anything you buy that you can't put on a credit card.

★ Buying what you don't need often ends up in needing what you can't buy.

★ Extravagance is buying whatever is of no earthly value to your wife.

★ Most husbands know what an extravaganza is. They married one.

Eloquence

★ Eloquence is the poetry of prose

F

Faith

* The Christian life is like an airplane — when you stop you drop!
* Dentists have more faith in people than anybody. It's a miracle that more of them don't get their fingers bitten off.
* No one has more faith than the person who plays a slot machine.
* Too much of the Christian faith has become trimming on the dress of life instead of a part of the fabric.
* A person's faith is not judged by what he says about it, but by what he does about it.
* Faith is to the soul what a mainspring is to a watch.
* All men need a faith that will not shrink when washed in the waters of affliction and adversity.
* Feed your faith and your doubts will starve to death.
* Faith keeps the man who keeps his faith.
* Faith builds a bridge from this world to the next.
* Faith is the daring of the soul to go farther than it can see.
* Faith is something like electricity. You can't see it, but you can see the light.
* Living without faith is like driving in a fog.
* When you pin your faith on some folks you ought to use a safety pin.
* Faith may move mountains, but only hard work can put a tunnel through.

Fast living

* If you burn the candle at both ends you are not as bright as you think.
* The higher you get in the evening, the lower you feel in the morning.
* Lots of people don't have to look at the the world through rose-coloured glasses — their eyes are already bloodshot.
* A slow day always follows a fast night.

★ You can't rise with the lark if you have been on one the night before.
★ Faith is an oasis in the heart which will never be reached by the caravan of thinking,
★ Faith is taking the first step even when you don't see the whole staircase.
★ Faith is the bird that feels the light and sings while the dawn is still dark.

Feedback

★ Feedback is the breakfast of champions.

Food

★ Most of us are too fond of people who agree with us and food that doesn't.
★ Don't argue at the dinner table. The one who is not hungry always wins the argument.
★ A child, like your stomach, doesn't need all you can afford to give it.
★ Nothing lasts as long as a box of cereal you don't like.
★ The trouble with square meals is that they make you round.
★ Health rule: Eat like a king for breakfast, a prince for lunch, and a pauper for dinner.
★ A girl can win a man with the smell of perfume, but she can't keep him without the smell of good food.
★ Happiness is like a potato salad — when shared with others, it's a picnic.
★ Table manners must have been invented by people who were never hungry.

Friends

★ Animals are such agreeable friends; they ask no questions, they make no criticisms.
★ The best antique is an old friend.
★ The more arguments you win, the fewer friends you'll have.
★ People make enemies by complaining too much to their friends.

★ The minute a man begins to feel his importance, his friends begin to doubt it.

★ We make more enemies by what we say than friends by what we do.

★ A friend will see you through after others see you are through.

★ Why not make friends before you need them?

★ Friends are like a priceless treaure; he who has none is a social pauper.

★ Friends last longer the less they are used.

★ God gives us our relatives, but thank heaven we can choose our friends.

★ A good friend is one who tells you all his problems — but doesn't.

★ A good friend is like a tube of toothpaste — comes through in a tight squeeze.

★ Don't make your friends a dumping ground for your troubles.

★ A friend is one who is there to care.

★ You can win more friends with your ears than with your mouth.

★ Friends are like radios — some have volume and some have tone.

★ The friends you make in prosperity are those you lose in adversity.

★ A true friend is one who sticks by you even when he gets to know you real well.

★ Friends are those who speak to you after others don't.

★ A good place to keep your friends is out of politics.

★ Prosperity makes friends; adversity tries them.

★ A loyal friend is someone who sticks up for you even when you're not there.

★ Treat your friends like a bank account — refrain from drawing too heavily on either.

★ Some friends are like your shadow — you see them only when the sun shines.

★ Hot tempers will mean cool friends.

★ Long tongue will mean short friends.

Friendship

★ The world needs more warm hearts and fewer hot heads.
★ Bees can't make honey and sting at the same time.
★ Always hold your head up, but be careful to keep your nose at a friendly level.
★ When a man borrows money from a bank he pays interest, but when he borrows from a friend he often loses interest.
★ Friendship is like money — easier made than kept.
★ The quickest way to wipe out a friendship is to sponge on it.
★ The world is round so that friendship may encircle it.

Future

★ It's better to look where you're going than to see where you've been.
★ Those who fear the future are likely to fumble the present.
★ The man who is afraid of his past may have reason to be afraid of his future.
★ Fear of the future is a waste of the present.
★ If we don't care for the future, the future won't care for us.
★ Hats off to the past, coats off to the future.
★ The future will be different if we make the present different.
★ There is no future in the past.
★ Don't take tomorrow to bed with you.
★ More people worry about the future than prepare for it.
★ The best thing to save for the future is your soul.
★ A kindness done today is the surest way to a brighter tomorrow.
★ A lie may take care of the present, but it has no future.
★ Man spends his life reasoning with the past, complaining about the present, and trembling for the future.
★ A pessimist burns his bridges before he gets to them.
★ Why worry about the future? The present is more than most of us can handle.

★ Go as far as you can see, and when you get there, you can see farther.

G

Girls

★ When a modern girl blushes she's probably been caught doing something proper.

★ Modern girls wear as many clothes as grandma, but not all at once.

★ A college girl may be poor in history, but great on dates.

★ Some college girls pursue learning and some others learn pursuing.

★ Cosmetics is used by teenage girls to make them look older sooner, and by their mothers to make them look younger longer.

★ Courtship is that part of a girl's life which comes between the lipstick and the broomstick.

★ The extravagant girl usually makes a poor mother and a bankrupt father.

★ It's amazing how many things a girl can do without until she gets married.

★ Any normal girl would rather be looked over than overlooked.

★ Some girls think it is better to be well-formed than well-informed.

★ A girl needs to keep on her toes to avoid heels.

★ Any girl can be glamorous. All she has to do is stand still and look stupid.

★ Some of our modern girls turn a man's head with charm — and his stomach with their cooking.

★ A girl can catch a man with face powder, but it takes baking powder to keep him.

★ When a girl is single, she's pensive. After she gets married, she's expensive.

★ Many girls are trying to break their boyfriends of a bad habit — eating alone.

★ A girl admires the tone of a bachelor's voice when there's a ring in it.

★ Any girl who knows how to cook can certainly find a man who knows how to eat.

★ Many of our modern girls have plenty of polish — on their fingernails

★ One of life's unsolved mysteries is what young girls giggle about.

★ Girls are like pianos. When they're not upright, they're grand.

★ Any girl can tell you that the only thing harder than a diamond is getting one.

★ There are three things most men love but never understand: females, girls, and women.

★ Football is popular with girls. They like to see men making passes.

Gossip

★ Nothing makes an argument so one-sided as telling about it.

★ Some people never say anything bad about the dead, or anything good about the living.

★ One nice thing about bores is that they don't talk about other people.

★ Conversation is when three women are talking; gossip is when one of them leaves.

★ Conversation between Adam and Eve must have been difficult at times because they had nobody to talk about.

★ Conversation is an exercise of the mind, but gossiping is merely an exercise of the tongue.

★ Envy is usually the mother of gossip.

★ Everybody should have at least two friends — one to talk to and one to talk about.

★ The quickest way to stop gossip is for everybody to shut up.

★ Gossip is always brewing at coffee break.

★ Gossip is nothing more than mouth-to-mouth recitation.

★ The only time some people dislike gossip is when you gossip about them.

★ A gossiper is a newscaster without a sponsor.

★ In most beauty parlours the gossip alone would curl your hair.

★ You can't believe everything you hear — but you can repeat it.

★ Gossip is like a balloon — it grows bigger with every puff.

★ Spreading gossip is impossible if we refuse to listen — or to believe it.

★ The difference between gossip and news is whether you hear it or tell it.

★ Gossip is what might be called, "ear pollution."

★ Nothing is dirt cheap anymore except gossip.

★ A gossip is a person with a strong sense of rumour.

★ Gossip is like grapefruit — it has to be juicy to be good.

★ Plant a little gossip and you will reap a harvest of regret.

★ A tongue four inches long can kill a man six feet tall.

Grandparents

★ A man begins to show his age at about the same time he begins to show pictures of his grandchildren.

★ Nothing makes a boy smarter than being a grandson.

★ Grandparents are people who come to your house, spoil the children, and them go home.

★ Another thing "so simple a child can operate" is a grandparent.

★ A grandmother is a baby sitter who watches the kids, instead of the television.

Gratitude

★ The greatest lesson we learn from past civilisation is ingratitude.

★ Our favourite attitude should be gratitude.

★ Debts of gratitude are the most difficult to collect.

★ Gratitude to God should be as regular as our heartbeat.

★ He who forgets the language of gratitude can never be on speaking terms with happiness.

★ Be grateful for what you have, not regretful for what you haven't.

★ Gratitude is not only the greatest of virtues, but parent of all the others.

★ Gratitude is the most exquisite form of courtesy.

★ No man is too big to be kind, but many men are too little.
★ Great minds have purposes; others have wishes.
★ The greater the man's talent, the more becoming his modesty.

Grumbling

★ When opportunity knocks a grumbler complains about the noise.
★ Some grumble because they don't get what's coming to them; others, because they do.
★ When you feel dog-tired at night, it may be because you growled and grumbled all day.
★ There is no place like home—where we are treated the best and grumble the most.

H

Habits

★ The worst boss anyone can have is bad habits.
★ Many girls are trying to break their boyfriends of a bad habit — eating alone.
★ The easiest and best way to break a habit is to drop it.
★ When a habit begins to cost money, it is called a hobby.
★ Good habits are usually formed; bad habits we fall into.
★ One can conquer a bad habit easier today than tomorrow.
★ We first make our habits, and then our habits make us.
★ A man spends the first half of his life learning habits that shorten the other half.
★ Form good habits; they're as hard to break as bad ones.
★ Habits are like a soft bed — easy to get into but hard to get out of.
★ Habit is a cable. We weave a thread of it every day until it is extremely difficult to break.

Happiness

★ For every minute you're angry, you lose sixty seconds of happiness.
★ A shady business never products a sunny life.
★ The happiest man in the world is a vegetarian looking at the prices in a meat market.

★ It seems that some people can't be happy unless they're unhappy.

★ The roots of happiness grow deepest in the soil of service.

★ Happiness is a place somewhere between *too much* and *too little*.

★ A small house will hold as much happiness as a big one.

★ Two things contribute to happiness: what we can do without and what we can do with.

★ Happiness is home-brewed.

★ The search for happiness is one of the chief sources of unhappiness.

★ Happiness is like the common cold — it's catching!

★ The heart is happiest when it beats for others.

★ Happiness is not something you have in your hands; it is something you carry in your heart.

★ The world would be happier if its leaders had more dreams and fewer nightmares.

★ Some pursue happiness — others create it.

★ Happiness is like a potato salad — when shared with others, it's a picnic.

★ Keep your happiness in circulation.

★ Happiness is in the heart, not in the circumstance.

★ Happiness does not come from what you have, but from what you are.

★ Basis for happiness: something to do, something to love, something to look forward to.

★ Happiness is getting something you wanted but didn't expect.

★ Happiness is not perfected until it is shared with others.

★ Wealth does not insure happiness, but neither does poverty.

★ Happiness will never come your way as long as your back is turned on duty.

★ It's not where you are but what you are that determines your happiness.

★ Happiness can never be found, because it was never lost.

★ Happiness is where you find it, and very seldom where you seek it.

Heart

★ Hardening of the heart ages people more quickly than hardening of the arteries.

★ It is not by the grey of the hair that one knows the age of the heart.

★ To change one's character, you must begin at the control centre — the heart.

★ The bigger the head, the smaller the heart.

★ Two things are bad for the heart — running upstairs and running down people.

★ The heart is happiest when it beats for others.

★ Happiness is not something you have in your hands; it is something you carry in your heart.

★ People take heart when you give them yours.

★ The most lonely place in the world is the human heart when love is absent.

★ Peace is not made in documents, but in the hearts of men.

★ It's not the body's posture, but the heart's attitude, that counts when we pray.

★ The smile that lights the face will also warm the heart.

★ There are many tears in the heart that never reach the eye.

★ Tears are the safety valves of the heart when too much pressure is put upon them.

Home

★ Children may tear up a house, but they never break up a home.

★ Among the best home furnishings are children.

★ Home is where you scratch anything that itches.

★ Home is where a fellow should hang his hat, not his head.

★ One nice thing about going home is that you don't have to make a reservation.

★ Money can build a house, but it takes love to make it a home.

★ Happy homes are built with blocks of patience.

★ In the grammatically correct home the wife says, "You shall," and the husband says, "I will."

★ There is no place like home if you haven't got the money to go out.

★ A house is made of walls and beams; a home is built with love and dreams.

★ Things would be a lot better if more folks at home felt at home.

★ Home is a place where women work in the absence of men, and men rest in the presence of women.

★ A typical home is where the TV set is better adjusted than the kids.

★ Like charity, obesity begins at home.

Husbands

★ A man hates to see a woman in cheap clothes, unless, of course, it's his wife.

★ Many a husband doesn't know a thing about women's clothes, except what they cost.

★ Most husbands would like for their wives to wear their dresses longer — about three years longer.

★ Sign in a florist's window: "Send flowers to the one you love. While you're at it, don't forget your wife."

★ Nothing makes the average wife so suspicious of her husband as an unexpected gift.

★ A husband controls his wife just like a barometer controls the weather.

★ A henpecked husband washes the dishes — even when they use paper plates.

★ Husbands are like sour pickles; the older they get, the sourer they get.

★ A husband often thinks he bosses the house — but actually he only houses the boss.

★ There are two kinds of husbands: one brings his wife a gift when he returns from a convention, and the other behaved himself.

★ A wise husband buys his wife fine china so she won't trust him to wash the dishes.

★ A husband is like an egg — if kept in hot water continually, he becomes hard-boiled.

★ Give some husbands enough rope and they'll skip.

★ Imagination is something that sits up with a wife when her husband comes home late.

★ Don't trust your wife's judgement — look at whom she married!

★ One of the problems of modern life is for a husband to teach his wife that even bargains cost money.

★ Some husbands quarrel with their wives, and others have learned to say, "Yes, dear."

★ Silence is a wife's best weapon. It upsets her husband.

★ The world's a stage all right, with husbands playing the supporting role.

Humour

★ Humour is the shock absorber of life; it helps us take the blows.

★ Humour is social lubricant that helps us get over some of the bad spots.

★ Laughter is a tranquiliser with no side effects.

★ What soap is to the body, laughter is to the soul.

★ The human race has one really effective weapon, and that is laughter.

★ Laughter is the shortest distance between two people.

★ Humour is a rubber sword- it allows you to make a point without drawing blood.

★ Comedy, we say, is society protecting itself – with a smile.

★ Wit is the salt of conversation, not the food.

★ Wit is like caviar-it should be served in small portions, and not spread about like marmalade.

I

Inflation

★ Airplane fares have been increased considerably. Even the cost of going up is going up.

★ Every year the cars get lower and wider, while the payments get longer and higher.

★ Inflated food prices are hard to swallow.

☆ Let's hope inflation flattens out before our wallets do.

☆ Inflation is when "never having it so good" never cost us so much.

☆ Inflation is the period when a fellow goes broke by just staying even.

☆ Inflation is when wallets are getting bigger and shopping bags are getting smaller.

☆ Thanks to inflation: it's costing more than ever to live beyond our means.

☆ Inflation is something like the flu — hard to trace and harder to stop.

☆ The more money is inflated, the less it can be stretched.

☆ The salary we used to dream of is the one we can't live on today.

Influence

☆ Every action of our lives touches some chord that will vibrate in eternity.

☆ Example is not the main thing in influencing others. It is the only thing.

☆ Please don't try to use your influence until you're sure you have it.

☆ One sure way for you to gain adherents to your cause is to start winning.

☆ It is impossible for you to influence others to live on a higher level than that on which you live yourself.

☆ Influence is something you think you have until you try to use it.

☆ Influence is like a savings account. The less you use it, the more you've got.

☆ A man lives as long as there are those who bear the stamp of his influence.

☆ Just one act of yours may turn the tide of another person's life.

☆ It's sad when a person has a head like a doorknob— anybody can turn it.

Instalment Plans

☆ Some people who buy modern furniture have antiques by the time they finish paying for it.

* Every year the cars get lower and wider, while the payments get longer and higher.
* The easiest way to lose control of a car is to forget to make the payments.
* Present-day cars are so quiet that the only noise you hear is from the finance company.
* Things bought on convenient terms always fall due at inconvenient times.
* A luxury becomes a necessity if we can make the down-payment on it.
* Many people don't do anything on time, except buy.
* Don't drive as if you owned the road — drive as if you owned the car.
* Life's greatest satisfactions include getting the last laugh, having the last word, and paying as the last instalment.
* Television is with us to stay — if we can keep up the payments.
* Time is what passes rapidly between the "easy monthly payments."

J

Jobs

* A man with a burning ambition is seldom fired.
* The best way to appreciate your job is to imagine yourself without one.
* Four word story of failure: Hired, tired, mired, fired.
* There is no future in any job. The future is in the man who holds the job.
* Stick to your job until one of you is through.
* The best time to start thinking about retirement is before your boss does.
* Ulcers are contagious. You can get them from your boss.
* Don't worry about the job you don't like. Someone else will soon have it.

Jokes

* Computers will never replace man entirely until they learn to laugh at the boss's jokes.

★ Real humour enables you to laugh when someone takes your best joke and improves on it.

★ Some husbands are living proof that a woman can take a joke.

★ If you can't remember a joke—don't dismember it.

★ Old jokes never die. They just smell that way.

★ You can judge a man not only by the company he keeps, but by the jokes he tells.

Judging

★ Be sure to judge yourself before you judge others.

★ Judge each day, not by the harvest, but by the seeds you plant.

★ Never judge a summer resort by its post cards.

★ Never judge a man by his relatives; he did not choose them.

★ Don't judge a man by the clothes he wears. God made one; the tailor, the other.

★ Never judge a man's actions until you know his motives.

★ We usually see things, not as they are, but as we are.

★ You can't always judge a dinner by the price.

Judgement

★ A man's judgement is no better than his information.

★ Don't condemn the judgement of another because it differs from your own. You both may be wrong.

★ The best some of us can expect on the Day of Judgement is a suspended sentence.

★ Your neighbour will seem like a better man when you judge him as you judge yourself.

★ The man who has a good opinion of himself is usually a poor judge.

Justice

★ Crime stories would be shorter if the sentences were longer.

★ Justice is what we get when the decision is in our favour.

★ There's justice for all, but it doesn't seem to be equally distributed.

★ Injustice is relatively easy to bear. What stings is justice!

K

Kisses

* ✶ Kissing a girl is like opening a jar of olives — hard to get the first one, but the rest comes easy.
* ✶ A kiss is a contraction of the mouth due to an enlargement of the heart.
* ✶ The word kiss is a word invented by poets to rhyme with bliss.
* ✶ It's nice to kiss the kids goodnights — if you don't mind waiting up for them.
* ✶ Kissing is a practice that shortens life — single life!

Knowledge

* ✶ Knowing without doing is like ploughing without sowing.
* ✶ A lot of good arguments are spoiled by some fool who knows what he's talking about.
* ✶ Discussion is an exchange of knowledge; argument is an exchange of ignorance.
* ✶ A college doesn't give you knowledge, it just shows you where it is.
* ✶ Heads that are filled with knowledge and wisdom have little space left for conceit.
* ✶ The chief benefit of education is to discover how little we know.
* ✶ Education should include knowledge of what to do with it.
* ✶ Education is not a head full of facts, but knowing how and where to find facts.
* ✶ The recipe for perpetual ignorance is to be satisfied with your opinions and content with your knowledge.
* ✶ Knowledge may have its limits — but not so with ignorance.
* ✶ Knowledge, like lumber, is best when well-seasoned.
* ✶ Knowledge has to be improved, challenged, and increased constantly or it vanishes.
* ✶ A smart person doesn't tell everything he knows, but he knows everything he tells.
* ✶ Firsthand knowledge does not become secondhand when used.
* ✶ Knowledge advances by steps, not by leaps.

★ Knowledge not put into practice is useless.
★ Some students drink at the fountain of knowledge. Others just gargle.
★ Knowledge is knowing a fact. Wisdom is knowing what to do with that fact.
★ The first step to knowledge is to know that you are ignorant.
★ You may know more than your employer, but his knowledge pays off.
★ Knowledge is like dynamite — dangerous unless handled wisely.
★ Money is like knowledge — the more you have, the less you need to brag.
★ Blessed is the man who does not speak until he knows what he is talking about.
★ Knowledge is knowing a fact. Wisdom is knowing what to do with that fact.
★ Wisdom is knowledge in action.
★ Knowledge can be memorised. Wisdom must think things through.
★ Zeal without knowledge is like heat without light.
★ Zeal without knowledge is fanaticism.
★ Zeal without knowledge is the sister of folly.

L

Language

★ We're using sign language more and more. We sign for just about everything we buy.
★ Never poke fun at someone who misuses and abuses the English language. He may be in training to write tomorrow's hit songs.
★ A man's language is an index of his mind.
★ A synonym is a word you use in place of one you can't spell.
★ Language is the dress of thought; every time you talk your mind is on parade.
★ Many people get unlimited mileage out of a limited vocabulary.

Laughter

★ Another thing learned in adversity is that a tyre isn't the only thing you can patch.

★ Much may be known of a man's character by what excites his laughter.

★ A man isn't really poor if he can still laugh.

★ Laugh and the world laughs with you; cry and the other guy has an even better sob story.

★ If you can laugh at it you can live with it.

★ Fortune smiles upon the man who can laugh at himself.

★ He who laughs last didn't get the joke.

★ Laughter is a tranquiliser with no side effects.

★ There is hope for any man who can look in a mirror and laugh at what he sees.

★ Laughter is the shock absorber that eases the blows of life.

★ A laugh is worth a hundred groans in any market.

★ If you're too busy to laugh, you're entirely too busy.

★ Laughter is the sweetest music that ever greeted the human ear.

★ Laughter is but a frown turned upside down.

★ Laughter is to life what salt is to an egg.

★ Try to make the world laugh; it already has enough to cry about.

★ Laugh and the world will laugh with you; think and you will almost die of loneliness.

★ Your ulcers can't grow while you're laughing.

Leaders

★ Education can't make us all leaders — but it can teach us which leader to follow.

★ If you're not afraid to face the music, you may someday lead the band.

★ The world would be happier if its leaders had more dreams and fewer nightmares.

★ Leaders go down in history — some farther down than others.

★ Don't ever follow any leader until you know whom he is following.

✯ A real leader faces the music even when he dislikes the tune.

✯ We herd sheep, we drive cattle, we lead men.

✯ Followers do not usually go any farther than their leaders.

✯ Leaders are ordinary people with extraordinary determination.

Liars

✯ A boaster and a liar are first cousins.

✯ A lot of people who boast they never go back on their word don't mind going around it a little.

✯ As a general rule, a liar is not believed even when he speaks the truth.

✯ A liar is one who forgets to keep a partition between his imagination and the true facts.

✯ A liar is hard not to believe when he says nice things about you.

✯ Some people are such liars you find it difficult to believe even the opposite of what they say.

✯ A liar is the type of person who gets the most enjoyment out of fishing.

Life

✯ Life is a verb, not a noun.

✯ Life is the art of drawing without an eraser.

✯ In life, as in football, you won't go far unless you know where the goalposts are.

✯ Life is a foreign language; all men mispronounce it.

✯ Life is like a very short visit to a toy shop between birth and death.

✯ Life is the game that must be played.

✯ Lives are like rivers; eventually they go where they must, not where we want them to.

✯ Life is like an onion: You peel it off one layer at a time, and sometimes you weep.

✯ Life is like a play: it's not the length, but the excellence of the acting that matters.

✯ There are chapters in every life which are seldom read.

★ Life is a rainbow which also includes black.

★ Life is a dream for the wise, a game for the fool, a comedy for the rich, a tragedy for the poor.

★ Life is like a taxi ride; the meter keeps ticking, whether you're getting anywhere, or just standing still.

★ Life is a journey, but don't worry, you'll find a parking spot at the end.

★ Life is a long lesson in humility.

★ Life is rather like a tin of sardines. We're all of us looking for the key.

★ Life is a grindstone, and whether it grinds a man down or polishes him up depends on what he is made of.

★ Life itself is the proper binge.

★ Life is like playing a violin solo in public and learning the instrument as one goes on.

★ Life is like music, it must be composed by ear, feeling, and instinct, not by rule.

★ Life is a tragedy when seen in closeup, but a comedy in long shot.

★ Life is a maze in which we take the wrong turning before we have learnt to walk.

★ Life is a sum of all choices.

★ Life is a game played on us while we are playing other games.

★ Life is a moderately good play with a badly written act.

★ Men deal with life as children with their play, who first misuse, then cast their toys away.

★ There are four steps to accomplishment: Plan purposefully, prepare prayerfully, proceed positively, pursue persistently.

★ Life is like riding a bicycle. To keep balance you must keep moving.

★ Life is like a ten-speed bicycle. Most of us have gears we never use.

★ Advice to some people: If you had your life to live over — don't do it!

★ Life not only begins at forty — it begins to show.

★ Men heap together the mistakes of their lives, and create a monster they call Destiny.

★ There are a lot of books telling you how to manage when you retire. What most people want is one that'll tell them how to manage in the meantime.

★ Life's heaviest burden is to have nothing to carry.

★ Drive with care. Life has no spare.

★ Death is not a period but a comma in the story of life.

★ Laughter is the shock absorber that eases the blows of life.

★ Life is like a camel — it won't back up.

★ If life is ever found on the planet Mars, they're certain to ask us for a loan.

★ Life is what you make of it until somebody makes it worse.

★ No one finds life worth living; he must make it worth living!

★ You cannot control the length of your life, but you can control its breadth, depth, and height.

★ Life is like a bank. You can't take out what you haven't put in.

★ The best things in life are free — plus tax, of course.

★ Life has become a struggle to keep our weight down and our spirits up.

★ Life is like a poker game — if you don't put anything in the pot, there won't be anything to take out.

★ Finding a way to live a simple life is today's most complicated job.

★ Life is 10 percent what you make it and 90 percent how you take it.

★ If your life is an open book, don't bore your friends by reading out of it.

★ Life is but a brief lull between the stork and the epitaph.

★ The best way to live a long life is to get somebody to do the worrying for you.

★ Life is an external struggle to keep money coming in and teeth, hair, and vital organs from coming out.

★ If you break the rules in the game of life, the rules will eventually break you.

★ So live your life that your autograph will be wanted instead of your fingerprints.

★ Life is like a mirror — we get the best results when we smile.

★ The best things in life are free — including the worst advice.

★ Life is like a radio comedy; it doesn't always follow the script.

★ There are three ingredients in the good life; learning, yearning, and earning.

★ Life is what you make of it, or what it makes of you.

★ Life is a cup to be filled, not drained.

★ Life would make more sense if we would live it backwards.

★ Life is like a mirror. If we frown at it, it frowns back. If we smile, it returns the greeting.

★ Life is full of golden opportunities for doing what we don't want to do.

★ The tragedy of life is what dies inside a man while he lives.

★ Life will lick you if you don't fight back.

★ The most important things in life aren't things.

★ Life has more questions than answers.

★ The tragedy of life is not that it ends so soon, but that we wait so long to begin it.

★ Many start life young and broke and wind up old and bent.

★ The world is full of people making a good living but poor lives.

★ Life is fragile — handle with prayer.

Liquor

★ Which do you suppose ages faster — whiskey or the man who drinks it?

★ An alcoholic claims a little too much liquor is just about right.

★ When we hear a man boasting about how much liquor he can hold, we get a mental picture of an animated garbage can.

★ Glasses can make driving a lot safer. Providing, of course, they're worn instead of emptied.

★ Dignity is one thing that cannot be preserved in alcohol.

★ The higher you get in the evening, the lower you feel in the morning.

- ★ A drunkard can live neither with alcohol nor without it.
- ★ If you drink too often to other people's health, you'll ruin your own.
- ★ Liquor is a lubricant only if a man is going downhill.
- ★ Whiskey improves with age, but those who drink it don't.
- ★ Some folks drink liquor as if they want to be mentioned in "BOOZE WHO."
- ★ Warning: Boozers are losers.
- ★ People who say that many things drive them to drink should walk.
- ★ Vodka is colourless, odourless, tasteless, and too much of it leaves you senseless.
- ★ Too many people attempt to fight the battles of life with a bottle.
- ★ Liquor is nothing but trouble in liquid form.
- ★ It's better to sit tight than to walk tight.
- ★ Nothing can hold liquor as well as a bottle — so why not leave it there?
- ★ Get the best of liquor or it will get the best of you.
- ★ When you come right down to it, the problem isn't alcohol — it's the people who drink it.
- ★ Drinking liquor is legal, but some people seem to think it's compulsory.
- ★ Glasses have an amazing effect on the eyes, especially after they've been emptied of liquor several times.
- ★ Many men give up drinking on account of the wife and bad kidneys.
- ★ It's when a man gets tight as a drum that he makes the most noise.
- ★ Liquor will not drown sorrows; it only irrigates them.
- ★ A "hangover" is something that occupies the head you neglected to use last night.
- ★ Anything can be pickled in alcohol. Just take a look at the guy next door!
- ★ Drinking is a subject that floors a lot of people.
- ★ If you drink enough moonshine, you won't see the sunshine.
- ★ Drinking to another man's health isn't going to improve your own.
- ★ Nothing can be more frequent than an occasional drink.

★ Four reasons for not drinking: the head is clearer, the health is better, the heart is lighter, and the purse is heavier.

★ Drinking is something that makes one lose inhibitions and give exhibitions.

★ The liquor of today is the hangover of tomorrow.

★ Some people drink when they have an occasion, and sometimes when they have no occasion.

★ A cocktail party is an excuse to drink for people who don't need any excuse.

★ If you drink like a fish, swim. Don't drive.

★ It takes only one drink to make a person drunk — and usually it's the fourth one.

★ There's one thing about whiskey — it always looks so sober in a glass.

★ Most people have no taste for liquor at all. They just gulp in down.

★ A drinking man is the last to be hired and the first to be fired.

★ The trouble with people who "drink like fish" is they don't drink what the fish drink.

★ A man is drunk when he feels sophisticated but can't pronounce it.

Love

★ Age is like love. It cannot be hidden.

★ Smoking cigars is like falling in love: first you are attracted to its shape; you stay with it for its flavour; and you must always remember never, never let the flame go out.

★ Love is friendship set on fire.

★ Love is like war: easy to begin but very hard to stop.

★ Love is like a virus. It can happen to anybody at any time.

★ Love is an exploding cigar which we willingly smoke.

★ Love is the wine of existence.

★ Memory is to love what the saucer is to the cup.

★ Love is the wild card of existence.

★ Love is a friendship set to music.

★ Love never dies of starvation, but often of digestion.

★ Love is a fan club with only two fans.

★ The world needs more warm hearts and fewer hot heads.

★ Love's like measles- all the worse when it comes late in life.

★ Love is like a cigar. If it goes out, you can light it again, but it never tastes quite the same.

★ You can always get someone to love you — even if you have to do it yourself.

★ Love is the quest, marriage the conquest, divorce the inquest.

★ A dog is the only thing on earth that loves you more than he loves himself.

★ Love looks through a telescope, envy, through a microscope.

★ In the language of flowers, the yellow rose means friendship, the red rose means love, and the orchid means business.

★ You can give without loving, but you can't love without giving.

★ Money can build a house, but it takes love to make it a home.

★ A house is made of walls and beams; a home is built with love and dreams.

★ Love is the glue that cements friendship; jealousy keeps it from sticking.

★ Kindness is the insignia of a loving heart.

★ The most lonely place in the world is the human heart, when love is absent.

★ To some people love is only the last word in a telegram.

★ Love is a little word; people make it big.

★ Nothing beats love at first sight, except love with insight.

★ "Puppy love" is just a prelude to a dog's life.

★ The sunlight of love will kill all the germs of jealousy and hate.

★ Love is sharing a part of yourself with others.

★ The most important thing a father can do for his children is to love their mother.

★ Those who deserve love least need it most.

★ Duty makes us do things well, but love makes us do them beautifully.

★ Love is like a vaccination — when it takes hold, you don't have to be told.

★ Love quickens all the senses — except common sense.
★ Love is more easily demonstrated than defined.
★ Love is the fairest flower that blooms in God's garden.
★ Love at first sight usually ends with divorce at first slight.
★ It's much wiser to love thy neighbour than his wife.
★ To love others makes us happy; to love ourselves makes us lonely.
★ There are three things most men love but never understand: females, girls, and women.
★ True love doesn't have a happy ending; true love doesn't have an ending.
★ Love is the only game in which two can play and both lose.
★ Love is disease you can't "catch" without being properly exposed.
★ Love is a fabric which never fades, no matter how often it is washed in the water of adversity and grief.
★ When you hear bells ringing, feel butterflies fluttering, and act as though you have bees in your bonnet — that's real love!
★ Love intoxicates a man; marriage often sobers him.
★ It's hard to keep a man's love with cold food.
★ Love is a ticklish sensation around the heart that can't be scratched!
★ A woman feels a man's love should be like a toothbrush. It shouldn't be shared.
★ Mother love is dangerous when it becomes smother love.
★ Works, not words, are the proof of love.
★ This will be a better world when the power of love replaces the love of power.

Luck

★ Choice, not chance, determines destiny.
★ A rabbit's foot is a poor substitute for horse sense.
★ Luck is a wonderful thing. The harder a person works, the more of it he seems to have.
★ Good luck is a lazy man's estimate of a worker's success.
★ Luck always seems to be against the man who depends on it.

★ Good luck often has the odour of perspiration about it.
★ Luck is good planning, carefully executed.
★ Industry is the mother of success—luck, a distant relative.

Luxuries

★ Advertising is what tells us which luxuries we can't do without.
★ Hate is a luxury no one can afford.
★ Laziness is a luxury that few people can afford.
★ Luxuries are what other people buy—not us!
★ Yesterday's luxuries are today's debts.

M

Marriage

★ Marriage is a bribe to make a housekeeper think she is a householder.
★ Marriage is like a bank account. You put it in, you take it out, you lose interest.
★ Marriage is a meal, with the dessert at the beginning.
★ Most accidents occur in the home. Many men use this as an excuse to stay out late.
★ Advertising is a good deal like marriage. There may be a better way, but what is it?
★ To the bachelor, horror films are pictures of a wedding.
★ A bachelor may have no buttons on his shirt, but a married man often has no shirt.
★ Courtship, unlike proper punctuation, is a period before a sentence.
★ When a man decides to marry, it may be the last decision he'll ever be allowed to make.
★ Judging by the divorce rate, a lot of people who said, "I do" — didn't.
★ Love is the quest, marriage the conquest, divorce the inquest.
★ Many divorces are caused by the marriage of two people who are in love with themselves.

★ Some men believe in dreams until they marry one.

★ A wedding cake is the only cake that can give you indigestion for the rest of your life.

★ Time separates the best of friends, and so does money — and marriage!

★ Girls who fall in love with a fellow at first sight sometimes wish they had taken a second look.

★ Some girls get married for financial security; others get divorced for the same reason.

★ Genuine happiness is when a wife sees a double chin on her husband's old girlfriend.

★ The honeymoon is a period of doting between dating and debating.

★ Husbands are like wood fires. When unattended they go out.

★ Marriage is like arthritis. You have to learn to live with it.

★ Most men think they're marrying a cook; most women think they're marrying a banker.

★ Marriage is perhaps the most expensive way to get advice for nothing.

★ In most marriages the husband is the provider and the wife is the decider.

★ The most difficult years of marriage are those following the wedding.

★ Too many people are finding it easier to get married than to stay married.

★ Marriage is the world's most expensive way of discovering your faults.

★ Before marriage the three little words are, "I love you." After marriage they are, "Let's eat out."

★ Getting married is like buying on credit. You see something, you like it, you make it your own, and you pay for it later.

★ Marriage is a case of two people agreeing to change each other's habits.

★ Marriage is like horse radish — men praise it with tears in their eyes.

★ The trouble with marriage is not the institution. It's the personnel.

★ When it comes to broken marriages most husbands will split the blame — half his wife's fault, and half her mother's.

★ Marriage is too often a process whereby love ripens into vengeance.

★ Marriages are made in heaven, but they are lived on earth.

★ To marry a woman for her beauty is like buying a house for its paint.

★ An engagement is an urge on the verge of a merge.

★ Nothing makes a marriage rust like distrust.

★ Marriage is too often a case where cupidity meets stupidity.

★ It takes at least two people to make a marriage — a single girl and an anxious mother.

★ Marriages are made in heaven — so are thunder and lighting.

★ One does not find happiness in marriage, but takes happiness into marriage.

★ Making marriage work is like operating a farm. You have to start all over again each morning.

★ A model marriage is one in which the wife is the treasure and the husband the treasury.

★ Women wear rings to show they're married, while men wear last year's clothes for the same reason.

★ Getting married is one mistake every man should make.

★ Marriage brings music into a man's life — he learns to play second fiddle.

★ Romance goes out the window when she stops knitting and starts needling.

★ Romance is like a game of chess — one false move and you're mated.

★ If a woman can be a sweetheart, valet, audience, cook and nurse, she is qualified for marriage.

★ A woman marries the first time for love, the second time for companionship, the third time for support, and the rest of the time from habit.

Men

★ Advice to men over fifty: Keep on open mind and a closed refrigerator.

★ By the time a man finds greener patures he's too old to climb the fence.

★ A man is usually as young as he feels but seldom as important.

★ Some people think the proper age for a man to start thinking of marriage is when he's old enough to realize he shouldn't.

★ Nothing age a man faster than trying to prove he's still as young as ever.

★ Few women admit their age. Few men act theirs.

★ Automobiles are like men — the less substantial they are, the more knocking they do.

★ Statistics show there are three ages when men misbehave: young, old, and middle.

★ Women's faults are many. Men have only two: everything they say and everything they do.

★ History records only one indispensable man — Adam.

★ A man is about halfway between what he thinks he is and what his secretary knows he is.

★ The man with PUSH will pass the man with PULL.

★ There are three kinds of men in the world: fits, misfits, and counterfeits.

★ There are a lot of men in this world who started at the bottom — and stayed there.

★ All men are born equal. The tough job is to outgrow it.

★ Some men grow; others just swell.

★ Men usually worry more about losing their hair than their heads.

Middle age

★ Youth looks ahead, old age looks back, and middle age looks tired.

★ Costmetics were used in the Middle Ages; in fact, they're still used in middle ages.

★ "Girls" is what women over forty-five call each other.

★ Life not only begins at forty — that's when it really begins to show.

★ They tell us that life begins at forty, but they don't say what kind of life.

★ Life may begin at forty, but so does rheumatism.

★ Middle age is that time of life when a woman won't tell her age, and a man won't act his.

★ Middle age is when you go all out and end up all in.

★ Middle age is when you can do just as much as ever — but don't.

★ Middle age is that time of life when you finally know your way around but don't feel like going.

★ One symptom of middle age is when the "morning after" lasts all day.

★ Middle age is that time of life when you convince yourself it isn't only a vitamin deficiency.

★ Middle age is when your memory is shorter, your experience longer, your stamina lower, and your forehead higher.

★ There are two ways to determine middle age — one is by calendar, and the other by the waistline.

★ Middle age is when a man's favourite nightspot is in front of a TV set.

★ One thing is certain about middle age — you wonder how you got there so fast.

★ In middle age it's difficult to decide what there's most of — middle or age.

★ When you begin to smile at things that once caused you to laugh, middle age is approaching.

★ You've reached middle age when your wife tells you to pull in your stomach, and you already have.

★ Middle age is when your clothes no longer fit, and it's not the clothes that need the alterations.

★ Middle age is when you start eating what's good for you, instead of what you like.

Money

★ There are a lot of hot arguments over "cold cash."

★ Perhaps the most necessary automobile accessory is a wallet.

★ By the time a man can afford to buy one of those little sports cars, he's too fat to get into it.

★ It is generally agreed that the first thing a new car runs into is money.

★ Having a big car doesn't always mean you have money; it may mean you once had money.

★ Married men can't understand why every bachelor isn't a millionaire.

★ The one book that always has a sad ending is a cheque book.

★ New shoes hurt the most when you have to buy them for the whole family.

★ Contentment is when your earning power equals your yearnings power.

★ Debts are about the only thing we can acquire without money.

★ Extravagance is anything you buy that you can't put on a credit card.

★ Nowadays the family that buys together cries together.

★ Fools sometimes make money, but money also sometimes makes fools.

★ Having money and friends is easy. Having friends and no money is an accomplishment.

★ A friend you can buy can be bought from you.

★ There are three faithful friends: an old wife, an old dog, and ready cash.

★ Friendship is like money — easier made than kept.

★ Money can build a house, but it takes love to make it a home.

★ The average man has more money than sense; the trouble is that he doesn't know it.

★ Inflation is when petty cash is the only kind there is.

★ Money will buy a fine dog, but only kindness will make him wag his tail.

★ Life is an eternal struggle to keep money coming in and teeth, hair, and vital organs from coming out.

★ Many people who suddenly realise that they can't afford to get married, already are.

★ Money not only changes hands — it changes people.

★ Dough is the wrong term for money. Dough sticks to your hands.

★ Money never did buy happiness, and credit cards aren't doing much better.

★ Many seem more concerned about making money than about earning it.

★ Nowadays everybody is putting their money where their mouth is — to kiss it goodbye.

★ The nice thing about money is that it never clashed with anything you're wearing.

★ Money may not be everything, but it's a pretty good cure for poverty.

★ The more money is inflated, the less it can be stretched.

★ Money is an ideal gift — everything else is too expensive!

★ Money isn't everything, but it does quiet the nerves a little.

★ Nothing makes money so useful as being yours.

★ We spend our lives trying to accumulate money, then look back to times when we had none and call them the "good old days."

★ Money doesn't really talk; it just makes a sonic boom as it goes by.

★ All our money these days is tied up in the market — the supermarket.

★ The love of money, and the tick of it, is the root of all kinds of evil.

★ Money can't buy love, health, happiness, or what it did last year.

★ When a man is broke he can count his friends on his thumb.

★ If you want to know the value of money, try and borrow it.

★ Our money talks today as if it were exhausted.

★ Money can't go to heaven, but it can do something heavenly here on earth.

★ Money will do more to you than it will do for you.

★ Hush money talks — and it also stops talk.

★ Money is like knowledge — the more you have, the less you need to brag.

★ There is one thing you can get without money — sick!

★ The best thing that parents can spend on their children is time — not money.

★ Success measured merely by money is too cheap.

Mothers

★ Mother love is dangerous when it becomes smother love.

★ A man is seldom as smart as his mother thinks, or as dumb as his mother-in-law says he is.

★ A mother who makes a match for her daughter usually intends to referee it as well.

★ Another reason for unhappy marriages is that men can't fool their wives like they could their mothers.

★ A mother should be like a quite — keep the children warm but don't smother them.

★ What a mother should save for a rainy day is patience.

★ Throughout the ages no nation has ever had a better friend than the mother who taught her children to pray.

★ A mother takes twenty-one years to make a man of her boy, and another woman can make a fool of him in twenty minutes.

★ A mother is a woman who decorates her life with babies.

★ A mother's patience is like a tube of toothpaste — it's never quite all gone.

★ There's only one perfect child in the world and every mother has it.

Mother-in-law

★ The penalty for bigamy is two mothers-in-law.

★ No man is really successful until his mother-in-law admits it.

★ "Double trouble" is a mother-in-law with a twin sister.

Movies

★ History does repeat itself, but not as often as old movies.

★ Just about the only people who still cry at the movies are theatre owners.

★ Once upon a time movies were rated on how good they were, not on who was allowed to see them.

★ In today's movies the theme is a dirty story, and the admission price is a dirty shame.

★ Maybe these movies with so much violence should be shown in black and blue.

★ Today's movies are either comedies or traumas.

★ The best way to stop kids from seeing dirty movies is to label them "Educational."

* The happiest ending in the movies is when the guy behind you finished eating his popcorn.
* Some of the movies of today should be pitied rather than censored.

MUSIC

* Is there any music as sweet as that of a car starting on a cold morning?
* The first thing a child learns when he gets a drum is that he's never going to get another one.
* Laughter is the sweetest music that ever greeted the human ear.
* Take time to laugh — it is the music of the soul.
* These days it's better to face the music than to have to listen to it.
* There is one good thing about today's popular music. If the acoustics are bad you don't know it.
* Marriage brings music into a man's life — he learns to play second fiddle.
* Music has been called medicine, and some of it is hard to take.
* The kind of music people should have in their homes is domestic harmony.
* It isn't facing the music that hurts these days; it's listening to it.
* Music is an attempt to express emotions that are beyond speech.
* Jazz music is an appeal to the emotions by an attack on the nerves.
* The trouble with country music is that it doesn't stay there.
* A folk singer is a guy who sings through his nose by ear.
* It seems that songs making the most money make the least sense.
* Nowadays what is not worth saying is sung.
* If you can write a song that's crazy enough your fortune is made.
* Many a violin sounds as though its strings were still in the cat.

☆ A violinist is always up to his chin in music.
☆ Much of our modern music makes you feel like clapping
your hands — over your ears!

Neighbours

☆ The only people who really listen to an argument are the
neighbours.
☆ Nothing depreciates a car faster than having a neighbour
buy a new one.
☆ Church is where you go to find out what your neighbours
should do to lead better lives.
☆ A contented person is one who has all the things his
neighbour has.
☆ The Bible admonished us to love our neighbours, and also
to love our enemies — probably because they are generally
the same people.
☆ It's so difficult to save money when your neighbours keep
buying things you can't afford!
☆ There should be music in every home — except the one
next door.
☆ A good neighbour is one who doesn't expect you to return
the things you borrow.
☆ The best neighbour is one who has everything you're out
of.
☆ If you have an unpleasant neighbour, the odds are that
he does too.
☆ A cooperative neighbour is one who advises you on what
to buy, so he can borrow it later.
☆ A good neighbour is a fellow who smiles at you over the
back fence but doesn't climb it.
☆ A neighbour is always doing something you can't afford.
☆ A neighbour likes to borrow your equipment and loan you
his troubles.
☆ "Love thy neighbour," but first be sure she isn't married!
☆ Poverty is often a state of mind induced by a neighbour
buying a new car.

News

☆ What a scarcity of news there would be if everybody
obeyed the Ten Commandments!

★ Current events are so grim that we can't decide whether to watch the six o'clock news and not be able to eat, or the ten o'clock news and not be able to sleep.

★ The difference between gossip and news is whether you hear it or tell it.

★ There are the days when we wish newscasters would cast their news somewhere else.

★ Most of today's news is too true to be good.

★ Not all the news that's fit to print is fit to read.

★ News is the same old thing — only happening to different people.

★ News makes the world very confusing. Some times it seems the Near East to too far, and the Far East is too near.

★ There are TV anchormen who receive twice as much money to read the news as the President gets to make the news.

Newspapers

★ Reading someone else's newspaper is like sleeping with someone else's wife.

★ A small town newspaper advertised, "Read Your Bible to know what people ought to do. Read this paper to know what they actually do."

★ Nothing improves a man's appearance as much as the photograph the newspapers use with his obituary.

★ Some men's names appear in the paper only three times: When they's too young to read, when they're too dazed to read, and when they're too dead to read.

★ Newspapers have reporters to write the news, columnists to misrepresent it, and delivery boys to throw it into your rosebushes.

★ A good way to get your name in the newspaper is to cross the street reading one.

★ A newspaper editor's business is to separate the wheat from the chaff and see to it that the chaff is printed.

★ Newspapers are owned by individuals and corporations, but freedom of the press belongs to the people.

★ A newspaper is a portable screen, behind which a man hides from the woman who is standing up in a bus.

★ Most newspapers condemn gambling on the editorial page and print racing tips on the sports page.

★ A newspaper is a circulating library with high blood pressure.

★ The radio will never take the place of the newspaper, because you can't swat flies with it.

★ It's not a bad idea for a politician to remember that no newspaper can misquote his silence.

★ One of the main differences in newspapers and television is that editors report violence. While TV producers create it.

O

Obesity

★ Many fat people have cut down to five cigarettes a day—one after each meal.

★ When some women show up in stretch pants, they sure do.

★ Always trust a fat man. He'll never stoop to anything low.

★ Most of our faults can be hidden, except overeating.

★ The trouble with square meals is that they make you round.

★ Like charity, obesity begins at home.

★ Overweight people don't like to hear four-letter words—such as diet.

★ Some folks go starch raving mad when they see food.

★ You're overweight when you begin living beyond your seams.

★ He who indulges bulges.

★ Everybody loves a fat man, but not when he has the other half of the seat on the bus.

★ Run out of places to hide it.

★ Obesity is surplus gone to waist.

Old age

★ By the time a man finds greener pastures, he's too old to climb the fence.

★ By all means go ahead and mellow with age. Just be wary of getting rotten.

★ Years make all of us old and very few of us wise.

★ The three ages of man are youth, middle age and, "My, but you are looking well."

★ By the time most folks learn to behave themselves they're too old to do anything else.

★ Children are a comfort to us in our old age, and they help us to reach it a lot sooner.

★ Years wrinkle the skin, but lack of enthusiasm wrinkles the soul

★ Experience is what you've got when you're too old to get a job.

★ We don't stop laughing because we grow old; we grow old because we stop laughing.

★ Old age is when most of the names in your little black book are doctors.

★ It's old age when each day makes you feel two days older.

★ The trouble with growing old is that there's not much future in it.

★ Old age has overtaken a man when he has to run to go as fast as he used to walk.

★ You can recognise the golden years by all the silver in your hair.

★ One nice thing about being old—as the noise level goes up, your hearing goes down.

★ It's wonderful to grow old, if you can remember to stay young while you're doing it.

★ You can tell you're getting old when you sit in a rocking chair and can't get it going.

★ The reason old folks enjoy living in the past is because it's larger then their future.

★ Old age is when you're willing to get up and give your seat to a lady—and can't.

★ Most women not only respect old age—they approach it with caution.

★ Old age is when you get enough exercise just trying to stay out of the way.

★ The best way to grow old is not to be in a hurry about it.

★ You have arrived at old age when all you can put in is your teeth into a glass.

★ The best thing about old age is that a person only has to go through it once.

★ Most old people enjoy living in the past. It's cheaper.

★ Old age is unpredictable. You just wake up one morning and you've got it!

★ Old age is when your idea of getting ahead is just to stay even.

★ Old age is something everybody else reaches before you do.

★ The worst thing about growing old is having to listen to a lot of advice from one's children.

★ When saving for old age be sure to lay up a few pleasant memories.

★ Some people will never live to be as old as they look.

★ It's funny how we never get too old to learn some new ways to be foolish.

★ By the time old people decide it's wise to watch their steps, they aren't going anywhere.

★ The only way to keep from growing old is to die young.

★ Three things indicate we are getting old. First, the loss of memory—and we can't remember the other two.

★ One of the nice things about old age is that you can whistle while you brush your teeth.

★ The trouble with life is that by the time a fellow gets to be an old hand at the game, he starts to lose his grip.

★ All some people do is grow old.

★ You are quite old if you can remember when children were strong enough to walk to school.

★ Old age is when the gleam in your eyes is just the sun shining on your bifocals.

★ The older a man gets, the less room he has in his medicine cabinet.

★ Old age is the only thing that comes to us without effort.

★ Grandchildren don't make a man feel old—it's knowing that he's married to a grandmother.

★ To keep young, stay around young people. To get old, try to keep up with them.

★ A sure sign of old age is when you feel your corns more than your oats.

★ Everybody wants to live a long time, but nobody wants to get old.

★ To avoid old age keep taking on new thoughts and throwing off old habits.

★ Old age is that period when a man is too old to take advice, but young enough to give it

★ We grow old not so much by living, but by losing interest in living.

★ Why do folks make such a fuss about growing old? All it takes is a little time!

★ If you're a senior citizen, don't try to keep up with the freshman class.

★ A woman is getting old when she feels insulted, rather than flattered, by a whistle.

★ Old age is a birthday cake where the candle power can't be overcome by wind velocity.

★ People may grow old gracefully, but seldom gratefully.

★ The best thing about growing old is that it takes such a long time.

★ About the only thing that comes to him who waits is old age.

★ You're getting old when the girl you smile at thinks you're one of her father's old friends.

Opinions

★ Most people, when they come to you for advice, want their opinions strengthened, not corrected.

★ People generally have too many opinions and not enough convictions.

★ Every man has a right to his opinion, but no man has a right to be wrong about the facts.

★ Facts do not change; feelings do.

★ A fanatic is one who can't change his opinions and won't change the subject.

★ There are two kinds of fools: those who can't change their opinions, and those who won't.

★ Always listen to the opinions of others. It may not do you much good but it will be better for them.

★ Public opinion is what folks think folks think.

★ Public opinion is private gossip which has reached epidemic proportions.

★ The quickest way to kindle a fire is to rub two opposing opinions together.

★ Public opinion is the greater force for good–when it happens to be on that side.

★ An opinion is often a minimum of facts combined with prejudice and emotion.

★ Public opinion is just private opinion that makes enough noise to be heard.

★ Prejudice is a great timesaver. It enables you to form opinions without bothering to get the facts.

★ One of the most difficult secrets for a man to keep is his opinion of himself.

Opportunity

★ There is far more opportunity than there is ability.

★ Good behaviour gets a lot of credit that really belongs to a lack of opportunity.

★ When opportunity knocks, a grumbler complains about the noise.

★ Sometimes it's difficult to know who's knocking–opportunity or temptation.

★ Opportunity never knocks at the door of a knocker.

★ It might not be opprtunity you hear knocking–it could be one of your relatives!

★ Life is full of golden opportunities for doing what we don't want to do.

★ Luck is what happens when preparation meets opportunity.

★ It's easier to open the door of opportunity after you have a key position.

★ A wise man will make more opportunities than he finds.

★ An opportunist hears opprtunity at the door before it knocks.

★ No business opportunity is ever lost. If you fumble your competitor will find it.

★ God makes opportunities, but He expects us to hunt for them.

★ Why don't we jump at opportunities as quickly as we jump to conclusions?

★ Life is full of hard knocks, but answer them all. One might be opportunity.

★ When you have a chance to embrace an opportunity, give it a big hug.

★ A great opportunity will only make you look ridiculous unless you are prepared to meet it.

★ Opportunities are often missed because we are broadcasting when we should be listening.

★ Never neglect the opportunity of keeping your mouth shut.

★ Even when opportunity knocks, a man still has to get off his seat and open the door.

★ Great opportunities come to those who make the most of small ones.

★ Many a man creates his own lack of opportunities.

★ The gates of opportunity swing on four hinges: initiative, insight, industry, and integrity.

★ Between tomorrow's dream and yesterday's regret is today's opportunity.

★ Weak men wait for opportunities; strong men make them.

★ In the orchard of opportunity, it is better to pick the fruit than to wait for it to fall.

★ Once an opportunity has passed, it cannot be caught.

★ The door of opportunity is opened by pushing.

★ Temptations, unlike opportunities, will always give you a second chance.

Parents

★ Adolescence is when children start bringing up their parents.

★ When a child pays attention to his parents, they're probably whispering.

★ A father is usually more pleased to have his child look like him than act like him.

★ An unusual child is one who asks his parents questions they can answer.

★ The only thing that children wear out faster than shoes are parents and teachers.

★ Children will be children—even after they are fifty years old.

★ Some children are running everything around the house, except errands.

★ Modern parents think children should be seen, not heard; children think parents should be neither seen nor heard.

★ What most children learn by doing is how to drive their parents almost crazy.

★ Christ was one child who knew more than His parents—yet He obeyed them.

★ Nowadays a parent can remember his son's first haircut—but not his last.

★ All a parent has to do to make a child thirsty is to fall asleep.

★ Parents are people who bear infants, bore teenagers, and board newlyweds.

★ Some parents begin with giving in and end with giving up.

★ The best thing that parents can spend on their children is time—not money.

★ The frightening thing about heredity and environment is that parents provide both.

★ Parents of children studying the "new math" not only don't know the answers, they can't even understand the questions.

★ The best inheritance parents can leave a child is a good name.

★ A father expects his son to be as good as he meant to be.

★ Child psychology is what children manage their parents with.

★ The creatures that sleep standing up are horses and fathers of one month old babies.

★ Nothing seems to make a wedding so expensive as being the father of the bride.

★ Once it was ambition that kept people on the move. Now it's no parking signs.

★ The nicest looking car is the one pulling out of a parking space you want.

★ Always look at the brighter side of things—whenever a car is stolen. It creates another parking place.

★ The course of true love never runs–it stops and parks!

People

★ No matter what you do, someone always knew you would.

★ There are two kinds of people in your church: those who agree with you and the bigots.

★ There are only two kinds of egotists–those who admit it and the rest of us.

★ God cares for people through people.

★ The person who looks up to God rarely looks down on people.

★ There is a mad scramble to improve just about everything in the world, except people.

★ Laugh with people–not at them.

★ When you laugh, be sure to laugh at what people do and not at what people are.

★ Money not only changes hands–it changes people.

★ There are some people who can't tell a lie, some who can't tell the truth, and a few others who can't tell the difference.

★ Many people are flexible. They can put either foot in their mouth.

★ People with a lot of brass are seldom polished.

★ When you give some people an even break they feel cheated.

★ The only time some people don't interrupt is when you're praising them.

★ It's not difficult to pick out the best people. They'll help you do it.

★ Many people would like to be respected without having to be respectable.

★ Have you noticed that many people have flat feet–and heads to match?

★ Nothing is something many people are good for.

★ It's too bad that more people are thoughtless than speechless.

★ A lot of people would pull their weight if some weren't so busy dragging their feet.

★ It is generally agreed that some people are wise and some otherwise.
★ It's so sad that people are like plants–some go to seed with age and others go to pot.
★ People who say they sleep like a baby haven't got one.
★ It's sad when a person has a head like a doorknob–anybody can turn it.
★ People are the main thing wrong with the world.
★ The world is full of people making a good living but poor lives.
★ Some people don't have enough push to go through a revolving door.
★ The only thing wrong with the world is the people.
★ The world is divided into people who do things and people who get the credit.

Physicians

★ Doctors and lawyers are always giving fee advice.
★ As a man gets older he suspects that nature is plotting against him for the benefit of doctors and dentists.
★ Never argue with your doctor; he has inside information.
★ You have a very common disease, if you're sick of high doctor fees.
★ If all men are born free, why doesn't somebody tell the hospitals and doctors about it?
★ One good place to study ancient history is in a doctor's waiting room.
★ A real hypochondriac is one who wants to be buried next to a doctor.
★ The lawyer agrees with the doctor that the best things in life are fees.
★ There's a shortage of doctors everywhere, except on TV.
★ The only way you can get a doctor to come to your home these days is to give a party.
★ A plastic surgeon increases your face value.
★ Most doctors specialise today–and the speciality of some is banking.
★ A consulting doctor is one who is called in at the last moment to share the blame.

★ The quickest way to get a doctor is to turn on the TV set.
★ A surgeon is a doctor who knows people inside out.

Politics

★ Money is the mother's milk of politics
★ Money is the crack cocaine of politics
★ Politics is the womb is which war develops.
★ You campaign in poetry. You govern in prose.
★ Everybody knows politics is a contact sport.
★ A government is the only vessel that leaks from the top.
★ Politics is the gizzard of society, full of gut and gravel.

Politicians

★ The occupational disease of politicians is SPENDICITIS.
★ People are not against political jokes–they just wonder how they get elected.
★ Politicians should watch their language–they use so much of it.
★ One thing about politicians–it's nice to know they can't all be elected.
★ Some of our politicians who act foolish aren't acting.
★ A politician is a man who never met a tax he didn't try to hike.
★ Political bumper stickers usually last longer than the politicians.
★ Politicians do more funny things naturally than most of us can do purposefully.
★ The cheaper the politician, the more he costs the country.
★ A good politician has prejudices enough to meet the demands of all his constituents.
★ Some politicians campaign for the funds of it.
★ Deceased politicians go to heaven and play harps. They're good at pulling strings.
★ Everytime a politician expresses a growing concern for something the price goes up.
★ Give a politician some facts and he'll draw his own confusions.
★ Politicians are the same all over the country. They promise to build bridges where there are no rivers.

★ Politicians should be good in geometry. They know all the angles and talk in circles.

★ Many a politician who considers himself farsighted is a poor judge of distance.

★ All politicians will stand for what they think the voters will fall for.

★ If the statements of opposing political candidates are true, none of them is fit to hold public office.

★ Another thing money can't buy is an honest politician.

★ Give a politician a free hand and he'll put it in your pocket.

★ Some politicians repair their fences by hedging.

★ The successful politician keeps on his toes all the time but never steps on the other fellow's.

★ A reawakening, it means he is running for office.

★ A politician is a fellow who's got what it takes to take what you've got.

★ Most politicians are continually running for office or for cover.

★ A politician hopes his platform will serve as a springboard to throw him into office.

★ Most politicians are both conservative and liberal–conservative with their own money, and liberal with ours.

★ Politicians fear that the young voters sill vote intelligently.

★ Politicians make headlines running for something or running from something.

★ A successful politician is one who can stay in the public eye without irritating it.

★ Politicians soon learn that many things done in the public interest don't interest the public.

★ Any politician will tell you the trick is to hit the taxpayer without hitting the voter.

★ Any political candidate will tell you that what this country needs is him.

★ Politics is too important to be left to the politicians.

★ Prosperity is something that businessmen create for politicians to take the credit for.

★ There are two sides to every question, and a politician usually takes both.

★ Most women keep secrets like politicians keep promises.

★ Too many of us spend our time the way politicians spend our money.

Power

★ Giving money and power to government is like giving whiskey and car keys to teenage boys.

★ Men of genius are admired; men of wealth are envied; men of power are feared; but only men of character are trusted.

★ You can kill men and cripple nations, but you cannot kill a good idea.

★ There is nothing in the world more powerful than an idea. No weapon can destroy it; no power can conquer it, except the power of another idea.

★ An idea is the only lever which really moves the world.

★ Knowledge is power only when it is turned on.

★ Power will either burn a man out or light him up.

★ The greatest power for good is the power of example.

★ There is more power in the open hand than in the clenched fist.

★ The power of man has grown in every sphere, except over himself.

Preparation

★ There are four steps to accomplishment:
Plan purposefully. Prepare prayerfully. Proceed positively. Pursue persistently.

★ Today's preparation determines tomorrow's achievement.

★ A lot of people who are worrying about the future ought to be preparing for it.

★ Luck is what happens when preparation meets opportunity.

★ Prepare and prevent instead of repair and repent.

★ When you're thirsty it's too late to think about digging a well.

★ Some folks prepare for an emergency before it emerges.

★ Hope for the best, and be ready for the world.

Progress

★ Begin where you are. But don't stay where you are.

★ Bees can't make honey and sting at the same time.

★ If everyone were perfectly contented there would be no progress.

★ Progress is seldom made without leaving somebody behind.

★ It is not enough to make progress; we must make it in the right direction.

★ The price of progress is change, and it is taking just about all we have.

★ The wheels of progress are not turned by cranks.

★ Progress is going around in the same circle—but faster.

★ Progress is largely a matter of discarding old worries and taking on new one.

★ Progress comes from making people sit up when they want to sit down.

★ The right train of thought can take you to a better station in life.

Promises

★ Promises may get friends, but it is performance that keeps them.

★ God makes a promise—faith believes it, hope anticipates it, patience quietly awaits it.

★ When liquor talks in a business deal, don't pin your faith on what it says.

★ Nothing stretches quite as far as a campaign promise.

★ A broken promise is one thing the best glue can't fix.

★ Promises are like crying babies in church—they should be carried out immediately.

★ A resolution is always stronger at its birth than at any subsequent period.

★ When you break your word, you break something that cannot be mended.

Public speakers

★ Some of the driest speeches are made by people who are all wet.

★ Many public speakers can talk for hours without any notes—or knowledge.

★ Public speaking is like eating salted peanuts. You have to know when to stop.

★ Some public speakers are guilty of podium pollution.

★ Why do so many speakers who want to be breezy end up windy!

★ There are two kinds of public speakers: one needs no introduction, the other deserves none.

★ A speaker ought to be the first person to know when he's through.

★ Many a public speaker who rises to the occasion stands too long.

★ To be a good speaker in public, you must be a good thinker in private.

Punctuality

★ Sign at an overseas airport: "Start kissing goodbye early, so the plane can leave on time."

★ Some folks are very punctual in always being late.

★ A great man once said that punctuality is the art of wasting only your own time.

★ One way a person can lose a lot of time is to always be on time for appointments.

Q

Quarrels

★ Quarrels would not last very long if the faults were only on one side.

★ Some husbands quarrel with their wives, and others have learned to say, "Yes, dear."

★ Too many people pick a quarrel before it's ripe.

★ When one will not, two cannot quarrel.

★ A quarrel is like buttermilk. The longer it stands, the more sour it becomes.

★ It takes two to make a quarrel and three to make it interesting.

Questions

★ An argument is a question with two sides–and not end.

★ An unusual child is one who asks his parents questions they can answer.

★ An expert knows all the answers–if you ask the right questions.

★ Women are to blame for men telling lies. They keep asking questions!

★ There are two sides to every question, and a politician usually takes both.

★ Where do kids get all those questions parents can't answer?

★ Anybody who thinks he knows all the answers just isn't up–to–date on the questions.

★ It is not every question that deserves an answer.

★ Modern youth is looking for new answers so they can question them.

Relatives

★ Anybody who has to ask for advice probably doesn't have any close relatives.

★ If a man's character is to be abused, there's nobody like a relative to get the job done.

★ After a good meal one can forgive anybody, even one's relatives.

★ God gives us our relatives, but thank heaven we can choose our friends.

★ Never judge a man by his relatives; he did not choose them.

★ It might not be opportunity you hear knocking–it could be one of your relatives!

★ In locating lost relatives, nothing succeeds like getting rich.

★ If the knock at the door is loud and long, it isn't opportunity. It's relatives.

★ The easiest way to make relatives feel at home is to visit them there.

★ A distant relative is not quite distant enough.

* The hardest thing to disguise is your true feelings when you put a lot of relatives on the plane for home.
* Everybody can use a rich and generous relative–and those who have usually do.
* Success is relative–the more success, the more relatives.

Religion

* The family altar would alter many a family.
* There is plenty of heavenly music for those who are tuned in.
* If your religion leaves your life unchanged, you'd better change your religion.
* Many people tailor their religion to fit the pattern of their prejudice.
* Religion costs, but irreligion costs more.
* You cannot prove your religion by its noise.
* Religion is like music–it does not need defence, but rendition.
* True religion is the life we live, not the creeds we profess.
* The world does not need a definition of religion as much as it needs a demonstration.
* The gospel of Jesus Christ breaks hard hearts and heals broken hearts.
* Arguing about religion is much easier than practicing it.
* A bitter world cannot be sweetened by a sour religion.
* Religion is no different from other things. The less you invest in it, the poorer the quality.
* It is never wise to argue about the religion you don't have.
* Religion is life. Faith is the only fuse.
* Some people carry their religion like a burden on their backs, when they should carry it like a song in their hearts.
* A man without religion is like a horse without a bridle.
* Religion at its best is a lift and not a load.
* Religion is not a way of looking at certain things. It is a certain way of looking at everything.
* It is a sad religion that is never strong, except when the owner is sick.

★ Religion is the best armour a person can wear, but it is the worst cloak.

★ If your religion means much to you, live so it will mean much to others.

★ Your religion will do more for you if you do more for it.

★ Quite often religion is like soap–those who need it most use it least.

★ Religion is like a bank–neither one pays dividends unless we make deposits.

★ The main object of religion is not to get a man into heaven, but to get heaven into him.

★ Religion doesn't fail. It's the people who fail religion.

★ "Kneeology" will do more for the world than theology.

★ If you hold your religion lightly you are sure to let it slip.

★ A bitter world cannot be sweetened by a sour religion.

Riches

★ Many girls are very romantic. They expect a declaration of love to have a ring in it.

★ How- to- get rich books are now filed under FICTION.

★ Be kind to people until you make your first million. After that people will be nice to you.

★ Being poor is a problem, but being rich isn't always the answer.

★ It's not a sin to be rich-it's a miracle!

★ It's better to live richly than to die rich.

★ Riches are often harder to manage than to acquire.

★ The futility of riches is stated very plainly in two places: the Bible and the income-tax form.

★ It is only after a man gets rich that he discovers how many poor relatives he has.

★ No amount of riches can atone for poverty of character.

★ Riches are a golden key that opens every door, save that of heaven.

★ In your search for riches, don't lose the things that money can't buy.

★ It is not what we *take up*, but what we *give up*, that makes us rich.

Romance

★ Fishing is like romance; the next best thing to experiencing it is talking about it.

★ Romance goes out of the window when she stops knitting and starts needling.

★ There's nothing like a marriage to break up a beautiful romance.

★ Sudden romances usually end the same way.

★ Romance often begins by a splashing water fall and ends over a leaky sink.

★ Nothing chills a romance like a cold shoulder.

★ A romantic fire is often kindled by a little spark in the park.

★ Romance is like a game of chess—one false move and you're mated.

S

Silence

★ A bit of advice: Say nothing often.

★ You must speak up to be heard, but sometimes you have to shut up to be appreciated.

★ In an argument the best weapon to hold is your tongue.

★ When a wise man argues with a woman, he says nothing!

★ So many books are now being written on how to speak that there ought to be a market for one on how to shut up.

★ If there is a substitute for brains it has to be silence.

★ Discretion is putting two and two together and keeping your mouth shut.

★ Wise men think without talking; fools reverse the order.

★ The quickest way to stop gossip is for everybody to shut up.

★ One of the best ways for some people to make others happy is to shut up and go home.

★ Speech is silver, silence is golden, and oratory, at the moment, is mainly brass.

★ More sales have been started when the salesman's mouth was closed than when it was open.

★ Try to understand silence—it's worth listening to.

★ Silence is what you can't say without breaking it.

★ An ounce of keep your mouth shut is worth a ton of explanation.

★ Often people who think before they speak don't speak.

★ Some people suffer in such silence it can almost deafen you.

★ The best way to say a thing is to say it, unless remaining silent will say it better.

★ It's better to be silent like a fool than to talk like one.

★ To be thought wise, keep your mouth shut.

★ Silence is often the most perfect expression of scorn.

★ Silence is the best and surest way to hide ignorance.

★ Don't repeat anything you will not sign your name to.

★ Most of us know how to say nothing, but few of us know when.

★ If men talked only about what they understand, the silence would be unbearable.

★ Another nice thing about silence is that it can't be repeated.

★ Very seldom can you improve on saying nothing.

★ The art of silence is as great as that of speech.

★ No flies ever got into a shut mouth.

★ If a thing will go without saying–let it.

★ The hardest thing to keep is quiet!

★ When a woman suffers in silence, she really does.

★ The best way to save face is to keep the lower half of it closed.

★ When at a loss for the right word to say–try silence.

★ An open mind and a closed mouth make a happy combination.

★ Silence has never yet betrayed anyone.

★ Women can do almost everything men can–except listen.

★ Nothing so excites a man's curiosity as a woman's complete silence.

★ When a woman suffers in silence, the phone is probably out of order.

★ Let's keep our mouths shut and our pens dry until we know the facts.

★ Silence is at its golden best when you keep it long enough to get all the facts.

★ You can think better if you close your eyes–and mouth.

★ A wise man is one who has an open mind and a closed mouth.

★ You can always tell a wise man by the smart things he does not say.

Sleep

★ The trouble with alarm clocks is that they always go off when you're asleep.

★ Conscience is like a baby. It has to go to sleep before you can.

★ The best tranquiliser is a good conscience.

★ Nothing goes to sleep as easy as one's conscience.

★ If you want your dreams to come true, don't oversleep.

★ Boasting and sleeping are the forerunners of failure.

★ If you count sheep two at a time you'll fall asleep twice as fast.

★ Sleep is something that always seems more important the morning after than the night before.

★ If you want your wife to listen to what you have to say, talk in your sleep.

★ Sound sleep is the sleep you're in when it's time to get up.

★ When a man walks in his sleep, he leaves his wife; when he talks in his sleep, his wife leaves him.

★ Sleep is a condition in which some people talk, some walk, and others snore.

Smiles

★ Your day goes the way the corners of your mouth turn.

★ Life is like a mirror. If we frown at it, it frowns back. If we smile, it returns the greeting.

★ Why not wear a smile? It's just about the only thing you can wear that isn't taxed.

★ One thing is certain—smiles never go up in price or down in value.

★ It's easy to smile when someone cares.

★ You're never fully dressed in the morning until you put on a smile.

★ A smile is a powerful weapon; you can even break ice with it.

⋆ Most smiles are started by another smile.

⋆ Smile now–you may not feel like it later.

⋆ The nice thing about wearing a smile is that one size fits everybody.

⋆ If you can look in the mirror and smile at what you see, there's hope for you.

⋆ A smile is the lighting system of the face and the heating system of the heart.

⋆ The ultimate in shapely curves is found within a smile.

⋆ Smile often and give your frown a rest.

⋆ When you meet a man without a smile, give him one of yours.

⋆ You know a woman is in love with her husband if she smiles at him the way she does at a traffic cop.

⋆ There are two things that everybody must face sooner for later: a camera and reality. A smile will help greatly in both instances.

⋆ The world looks brighter from behind a smile.

⋆ One smile in public is worth ten before your mirror.

⋆ A smile is the same in all languages.

⋆ If there is a smile in your heart, your face will show it.

⋆ Another smile does not make the giver poorer, but it does enrich the receiver.

⋆ A smile is the light in the window of your face that tell people you're at home.

⋆ People seldom notice old clothes if you wear a big smile.

⋆ The smile that lights the face will also warm the heart.

⋆ *Smiles* is the longest word in the world. There's a *"mile"* between the first and the last letters in the word.

⋆ A pleasant smile brings the largest return on the smallest investment.

⋆ It takes twenty-six muscles to smile and sixty-two muscles to frown. Why not make it easy on yourself?

⋆ A smile is mightier than a grin!

⋆ It is almost impossible to smile on the outside without feeling better on the inside.

⋆ A smile is a curve that can set a lot of things straight.

⋆ The only thing you can wear that's never out of style is a smile.

⋆ A smile is the shortest distance between two people.

★ A smile is the magic language of diplomacy that even a baby understands.

★ A smile is a curve that you throw at another, and it always results in a hit.

★ The world always looks brighter from behind a smile.

Sports

★ In life, as in a football game, the principle to follow is: hit the line hard.

★ Football is about as close as you can get to war and still remain civilised.

★ Boxing is just showbiz with blood.

★ Sports is the toy department of life.

★ A tie is like kissing your sister.

★ Golf is a puzzle without an answer.

★ Bridge is a sport of the mind.

★ Baseball is like church. Many attend, but few understand.

★ Running is the greatest metaphor for life, because you get out of it what you pour into it.

Success

★ If you're going to climb, you've got to grab the branches, not the blossoms.

★ The man who gets ahead is the man who does more than is necessary–and keeps on doing it.

★ The fellow who does things that count doesn't usually stop to count them.

★ Our ship would come in much sooner if we'd only swim out to meet it.

★ The lines actors like best are the ones in front of the box office.

★ Business is made good by yearning, learning, and earning.

★ The difference between failure and success is doing a thing almost right and doing it exactly right.

★ Failure always catches up with those who sit down and wait for success.

★ A man hopes that his lean years are behind him; a woman, that hers are ahead.

★ Good luck is a lazy man's estimate of a worker's success.

★ The average man doesn't usually increase his average.

★ An upright man can never be a downright failure.

★ Success in marriage is more than finding the right person. It's also a matter of being the right person.

★ The secret of success is seldom well-kept.

★ Skiing is one major sport where success involves starting at the top and working your way down.

★ No man is really successful until his mother-in-law admits it.

★ There are two elements of success: aspiration and perspiration.

★ Success measured merely by money is too cheap.

★ To succeed–keep your head up and your overhead down.

★ A successful man continues to look for work after he has found a job.

★ Don't forget the folks who are holding the ladder while you're climbing to success.

★ Success is relative–the more success, the more relatives.

★ Behind every successful man there are usually a lot of unsuccessful years.

★ You're not successful till someone brags they sat beside you in grade school.

★ If at first you don't succeed, try trying.

★ Success that goes to a man's head usually pays a very short visit.

★ For success, try aspiration, inspiration, and perspiration.

★ Success is like an underwear. We should have it without showing it off.

★ Forget the past; no man has yet backed into success.

★ The shortest route to success is the straight road.

★ Formula for success: When you start a thing, finish it.

★ The dictionary is the only place where success comes before work.

★ There isn't any map on the road to success. You have to find your own way.

★ Success is sweet, but its secret is sweat.

★ No one has yet climbed the ladder of success with his hands in his pockets.

★ God gave to man five senses: touch, taste, smell, sight, and hearing. The successful man has two more–horse and common.

★ He has achieved success who has lived long, laughed often, and loved much.

★ If you itch for success, keep on scratching.

★ Most people do only what they are required to do, but successful people do a little more.

★ The road to success is dotted with many tempting parking spaces.

★ To succeed you must be easy to start and hard to stop.

★ If at first you don't succeed, find out why before you try again.

★ A formula for success in bureaucracy: shoot the bull, pass the buck, and make seven copies of everything.

★ Success consists of doing the common things of life uncommonly well.

★ Any person who looks happy when he isn't is well on the road to success.

★ Even the woodpecker has discovered that the only way to succeed is to use one's head.

★ One thing that keeps a lot of people from being a success is work.

★ Success depends partly on whether people like you wherever you go or whenever you go.

★ There are no shade trees on the road to success.

★ If you want to succeed, wear out two pairs of shoes to every suit.

★ There are many keys to success, but they keep changing the lock.

★ Few people travel the road to success without a puncture or two.

★ Industry is the mother of success–luck, a distant relative.

★ To reach the front many a man has to be kicked in the rear.

★ The road to success runs uphill. So don't expect to break any speed records.

★ Be careful where you inquire for directions along the road of success.

★ No one has ever travelled the road to success on a pass.
★ The road to success is filled with women pushing their husbands along.
★ The secret of success is to start from scratch and keep on scratching.
★ There is really no such thing as the "ladder of success." It's a greased pole.

Skyscrapers

★ A skyscraper is a boast in glass and steel.
★ A skyscraper is in architecture as a boast is in interpersonal relations.

T

Talking

★ It isn't so much what we say as the number of times we say it that makes us a bore.
★ What the church needs is more men who talk less and work more.
★ When all is said and nothing done, it's time for the conference to adjourn.
★ A dog is smarter than some people. It wags its tail and not its tongue.
★ We make more enemies by what we say than friends by what we do.
★ About the only part of the body that is over-exercised is the lower jaw.
★ Fishing is like romance; the next best thing to experiencing it is talking about it.
★ Among the most expensive gifts on earth is the gift of the gab.
★ Intelligence is like a river–the deeper it is, the less noise it makes.
★ Kindness has influenced more people than eloquence.
★ Talk is cheap because the supply always exceeds the demand.
★ Everybody wants to talk, few want to think, and nobody wants to listen.

★ Talking too much usually follows thinking too little.

★ Two many people are like buttons — always popping off at the wrong time.

★ A lot of people have the gift of the gab; others have the gift of grab.

★ The best way to save face is to stop shooting it off.

★ Some women work their tongues so fast they say things they haven't even thought of yet.

★ Many people who have the gift of the gab don't seem to know how to wrap it up.

★ Some people have eyes that see not and ears that hear not, but there are very few people who have tongues that talk not.

Teachers

★ Education pays less when you are an educator.

★ Education helps you earn more. But not many school teachers can prove it.

★ Experience is the best teacher, and considering what it costs, it should be.

★ One reason experience is such a good teacher is that she doesn't allow any dropouts.

★ Another reason why experience is the best teacher–she is always on the job.

★ School teachers are given too much credit and too little cash.

★ It's not so much what is poured into the student, but what is planted, that really counts.

★ The world seldom notices who the teachers are; but civilisation depends on what they do and what they say.

Tears

★ As soap is to the body, tears are to the soul.

★ Laugh and he world laughs with you; cry and the other guy has an even better sob story.

★ Sometimes we get the feeling we laugh by the inch and cry by the yard.

★ There are many tears in the heart that never reach the heart.

★ Nothing dries quicker than a tear.
★ A woman's tears are the greatest waterpower known to man.
★ Tears are the safety valves of the heart when too much pressure is put upon them.
★ When a woman resorts to tears, she's either trying to get something out of her system or out of her husband.

Time

★ Light tomorrow with today.
★ The best thing to spend on children is your time.
★ A committee usually keeps minutes and wastes hours.
★ The best thing that parents can spend on their children is time–not money.
★ The easiest way to find more time to do all the things you want to do is to turn off the television.
★ Killing time is not murder, it's suicide.
★ Our birthdays are feathers in the broad wing of time.
★ Everybody, soon or late, sits down to a banquet of consequences.
★ Time is so powerful it is given to us only in small quantities.
★ When you kill time, just remember it has no resurrection.
★ Nothing makes time pass faster than vacations and short-term loans.
★ Time is what we want the most, and what we use the worst.
★ Counting time is not nearly as important as making time count.
★ Time may be a great healer, but it's no beauty specialist.
★ Today is the tomorrow you worried about yesterday.
★ Time waits for no man–but it stands still for a woman of thirty-five!
★ Hours and flowers soon fade away.
★ Lost time is never found again.
★ Time can be wasted but never recycled.
★ The only person who saves time is the one who spends it wisely.
★ Father Time grants no rebate for wasted hours.
★ The person who kills time hasn't learned the value of life.

U

Unemployment

* ★ If some folks aren't careful, they'll stretch their coffee break to the unemployment office.
* ★ Any girl who wants to be sure she will never be unemployed should marry a farmer.
* ★ Old Satan has no unemployment problems.
* ★ The army of the unemployed seems to have a lot of volunteers.

V

Values

* ★ We must cultivate our garden.
* ★ There are two ways of spreading light: to be the candle, or the mirror that reflects it.
* ★ We boil at different degrees.
* ★ A Bible stored in the mind is worth a dozen stored in the bottom of a trunk.
* ★ A good deed gets about as much attention these days as a homely face.
* ★ Don't call it education unless it has taught you life's true values.
* ★ Be slow in choosing friends, slower in changing them.
* ★ Money can build a house, but it takes love to make it a home.
* ★ A man doesn't know the value of a woman's love until he starts paying alimony.
* ★ Plenty in the purse cannot prevent starvation in the soul.
* ★ The things of greatest value in life are those things that multiply when divided.

Vices

* ★ More people are flattered into virtue than bullied out of vice.
* ★ Vice of any kind must become respectable before it is dangerous.

★ Vices are to be condemned and eradicated, not condoned and taxed for revenue.

★ Man's greatest vices are the misuses of his virtues.

Vision

★ It's better to look where you're going than to see where you've been.

★ Conceit is a form of "I" strain that doctors can't cure.

★ Faith is the daring of the soul to go farther than it can see.

★ Carrots are definitely good for the eyes. Have you ever seen a rabbit with glasses?

★ We usually see things, not as they are, but as we are.

★ The world could certainly use more vision and less television.

W

Weddings

★ To the bachelor, horror films are pictures of a wedding.

★ The best and surest way to save a marriage from divorce is not to show up for the wedding.

★ Give a girl enough rope and she'll ring the wedding bell.

★ Most girls seem to marry men like their fathers. maybe that's the reason so many mothers cry at weddings.

★ Nothing seems to make a wedding so expensive as being the father of the bride.

★ Some people never go to a wedding. They can't stand to see a man deprived of his human rights.

★ It's unlucky to postpone a wedding, but not if you keep on doing it.

★ People cry at weddings because they have been through it and know it's no laughing matter.

Wives

★ A man whose actions leave his wife speechless has really done something!

★ Advertising can be very expensive, especially if your wife can read.

* The argument you just won with your wife isn't over yet.
* A man hates to see a woman in cheap clothes, unless, of course, it's his wife.
* The best way to compliment your wife is frequently.
* The safest way to disagree with your wife is very quietly.
* A flimsy excuse is one that your wife can see through.
* When a man is generous, the last one to find it out is usually his wife.
* Genuine happiness is when a wife sees a double chin on her husband's old girlfriend.
* Many a husband comes home from work and hopes the kitchen stove is as warm as the TV set.
* There are two reasons why husbands leave home–wives who can cook and won't, and wives who can't cook and do.
* Imagination is something that sits up with a wife when her husband comes home late.
* Husbands lay down the law, but wives usually repeal it.
* Most women don't buy life insurance–they marry it.
* A man may be drinking because his wife walked out on him–or because she walked in on him.
* A husband knows his wife loves him when she returns a dress he can't afford.
* The man who gets his money the hard way is the one who has to ask his wife for it.
* The successful man has a wife who tells him what to do, and a secretary who does it.
* The road to success is filled with women pushing their husbands along.
* If you think you have trouble supporting a wife, just try not supporting her!
* Vacations are easy to plan–the boss tells you when, and the wife tells you where.
* A good wife and good health are a man's best wealth.
* The handiest thing a wife can have at her fingertips is a good husband.
* There's only one thing more expensive than a wife–an ex–wife!
* The best thing about some men is their wives.
* A man may be able to read his wife like a book, but he can't shut her up like one.

* The one thing that proves you can't afford to support a wife is having one.
* Many a wife leads a double life–hers and his.
* The economical wife is one who uses only thirty candles on her fortieth birthday cake.
* Candy and flowers may serve-one of two purposes–they make a wife happy or suspicious.
* No man should tell his wife anymore than he wants to be reminded of later.
* Many wives have a wonderful way to make a long story short–they interrupt.
* The trouble with modern wives is that they'd rather mend your ways than your socks.
* It is well for a girl with a future to avoid the man with a past.
* The best way to stop smoking cigarettes is to marry a woman who objects to it.
* The nicest things in men's clothing are women.
* What the well-dressed woman is wearing this year is less.
* Men no longer hide behind women's skirts; neither do women.
* Cosmetics were used in the Middle Ages; in fact, they're still used in the middle ages.
* Cosmetics are a woman's hope of keeping men from reading between the lines.
* Generally, women don't like the dictionary, because it has the first and the last word.
* Most women don't buy life insurance–they marry it.
* There are three things most men love but never understand: females, girls, and women.
* A woman feels a man's love should be like a toothbrush. It shouldn't be shared.
* Every man has three secret wishes–to outsmart racehorses, women, and fish.
* Some women have a terrible memory–they remember everything!
* Middle age is that time of life when a woman won't tell her age, and a man won't act his.
* A woman's mind is like the moon. No matter how often she changes it, there's always a man in it.

★ All women don't nag. Some aren't married.
★ Men's troubles are largely due to three things: women, money–and both.
★ A woman will go to almost any length to change her width.
★ If a woman can be a sweetheart, valet, audience, cook, and nurse, she is qualified for marriage.
★ Time and tide waits for no man–but a woman will.
★ It does not take a very bright woman to dazzle some men.
★ A middle-aged woman is one too young for Medicare and too old for men to care.
★ Even if a man could understand women, he still wouldn't believe it.
★ Some women grow old gracefully–others wear stretch pants.

Words

★ Words are, of course, the most powerful drug used by mankind.
★ Words are the physician of a mind diseased.
★ Actions speak louder than words–and speak fewer lies.
★ Kind words can never die, but without kind deeds they can sound mighty sick.
★ An argument is where two people are trying to get in the last word first.
★ It is much wiser to choose what you say than to say what you choose.
★ A dictionary is a guide to the spelling of words–provided you know how to spell them.
★ A lot of indigestion is caused by people having to eat their own words.
★ Let all your words be kind, and you will always hear kind echoes.
★ Never part without loving words. They might by your last
★ Works, not words, are the proof of love.
★ Kind words are short to speak, but their echoes are endless.
★ It takes only a few words mumbled in church and you're married. It takes only a few words mumbled in your sleep and you're divorced.

* What makes eating your words so difficult is swallowing your pride at the same time.
* Words can make a deeper scar than silence can ever heal.
* A kind word picks up a man when trouble weighs him down.
* Words and feathers are easily scattered, but not easily gathered up.
* The three most difficult words to speak are, "I was mistaken."
* *Right* is a bigger word than either success or failure.
* Luck is a wonderful thing. The harder a person works, the more of it he seems to have.
* Selling is quite easy if you work hard enough at it.
* Behind every successful man there are usually a lot of unsuccessful years.
* You don't have to lie awake nights to succeed; just stay awake days.
* Industry is the mother of success–luck, a distant relative.
* The only thing you can get without work is debt.
* Hard work never hurts people who don't do any.
* A few people are enthusiastic about work, but most of the time they're the bosses.
* Work isn't work if you like it.
* Hard work is the yeast that raises the dough.
* Work is the meat of life; pleasure, the dessert.
* One way to boost production in this country would be to put the labour bosses to work.
* Human beings, like chickens, thrive best when they have to scratch for what they get.
* If hard work is the key to success, most people would rather pick the lock.
* Faith may move mountains, but only hard work can put a tunnel through.
* Work is the best thing ever invented for killing time.

World

* After a man makes his mark in the world, a lot of people will come around with an eraser.

★ Friendship is the only cement that will hold the world together.

★ A lot of people are worrying about the future of the world, as though it had one.

★ In a world where death is, we should have no time to hate.

★ By improving yourself the world is made better.

★ The world is a book, and those who do not travel read only one page.

★ If the world laughs at you, laugh right back–it's as funny as you are.

★ The biggest problem in the world could have been settled when it was small.

★ Thoughts rule the world.

★ Why not take the world as it is, not as it should be.

★ All the world lives in two tents: content and discontent.

★ "All the world is a stage," and most of us are under – rehearsed.

★ The world always looks brighter from behind a smile.

★ If the world is a stage, it's putting on a mighty poor show.

★ Give the world what it needs and it will supply yours.

★ The world's a stage all right, with husbands playing the supporting role.

★ A bitter world cannot be sweetened by a sour religion.

Writing

★ Writing is thinking on paper.

★ Writing a novel is like building a wall brick–by–brick; only amateurs believe in inspiration.

★ Authors are actors, books are theatres.

★ Writing is easy. You must sit down at the typewriter, open up a vein, and bleed it out drop–by–drop.

★ In literature as in love we are astonished at what is chosen by others.

★ Liking a writer and then meeting the writer is like liking the goose liver and then meeting the goose.

★ Being a writer is like having homework every night for the rest of your life.

★ Footnotes- little dogs yapping at the heel of the text.

★ Writing a novel, like making chicken soup or making love,

is an idiosyncratic occupation; probably no two people do it the same way.

★ Prose is architecture, not interior decoration.

★ The most technologically – efficient machine that man has ever invented is the book.

★ Word carpentry is like any other carpentry: you must join your sentences smoothly.

★ Writing is manual labour of the mind; a job, like laying pipe.

★ To read without reflecting is like eating without digesting.

★ Writing is simply thinking though fingers.

★ Talent is like a faucet, while it is open, one must write.

★ When you get the itch of poetry, scratch your pen.

★ All good writing is swimming under water and holding your breath.

Y

Yawns

★ Advertising is what transforms a yawn into a yearn.

★ Home is a place where you don't have to stifle a yawn and try to cover it up with a smile.

★ The safest way to spend a holiday is to sit at home and yawn.

★ There is one protest sign that is understood the world over—a stifled yawn.

★ A yawn is sometimes a silent yawn.

★ A yawn may not be polite, but it lets everybody know how you feel.

Youth

★ Age is the best possible fire extinguisher for flaming youth.

★ Youth and beauty fade; character endures forever.

★ In youth we run into difficulties. In old age difficulties run into us.

★ The accent may be on youth these days, but the stress is still on the parents.

★ Old men declare wars, but it is youth that must fight them.

☆ A misspent youth may result in a tragic old age.
☆ Youth is like fashion. Both fade quickly.
☆ Youth isn't satisfied with a new deal–they want the whole deck.
☆ Young folks of today have the disadvantage of having too many advantages.

Z

Zeal

☆ The cross is easier to the Christian who takes it up than to the one who drags it along.
☆ He who has no fire in himself cannot warm.
☆ Zeal without knowledge is like heat without light.
☆ Zeal without knowledge is fanaticism.
☆ Zeal without knowledge is the sister of folly.

Potpourri

★ A fool and his money are soon invited places.

★ An optimistic gardener is a person who believes that what goes down must come up.

★ Most of our time is taken up making good, making trouble, or making excuses.

★ It's not too hard to live with your own faults, but it's hard to put up with the faults of others.

★ The guy we don't like is the one who is always me-deep in conversation.

★ A luxury is something you don't need but feel you can't do without.

★ Nowadays no farmer counts his chickens till they cross the road.

★ The fellow who embezzles the money always seems calm and collected.

★ One advantage in being stupid is that you don't get lonesome.

★ No one worries now about the wolf at the door as long as you can feed him on instalment plan.

★ If we could see ourselves as others see us, we would never want a second look.

★ Some folks speak when they think and some oftener.

★ There has been only one indispensable man, and that was Adam.

★ The family that isn't in debt today is underprivileged.

★ When you go on a vacation to forget everything, you generally find when you open your bag at the hotel that you have.

★ The young man in love thinks nothing is good enough for the girl except himself.

★ Early to bed and early to rise, and you'll miss hearing and seeing a great deal that would make you wise.

★ A sure way to keep crime from paying is to let the government run it.

★ Things are pretty well evened up in this world. Other people's troubles are not as bad as yours, but their children are a lot worse.

★ A chip on the shoulder is about the heaviest load a person ever carries.

★ Travel flattens the purse, broadens the mind, and lengthens the conversation.

★ To train children at home, it is necessary for both parents and children to spend some time there.

★ Most girls prefer the strong, solvent type.

★ Some persons are the kind of friends who stand by you— with their arms folded.

★ The bridegroom fainted on the way to his wedding. Wait till he gets the first month's bills.

★ A nation needs a foreign policy that isn't patterned after its weather policy.

★ Strangely, the less you see of some persons, the more you like them.

★ A pessimist is an optimist who voted for a politician he thought would reduce government spending.

★ A fashion note says that there will be little change in men's pockets during the next year.

★ By the time you get enough experience to be able to watch your step, you may not be going anywhere.

★ You can lose your shirt by putting too much on the cuff.

★ More people would try to do right if they thought it was wrong.

★ A business recession is when you do without some necessities in order to keep on buying your usual luxuries.

★ A brilliant conversationalist is a person who uses meaningless words to say a great deal about nothing.

★ The products are seldom as irritating as the commercials.

★ If you don't know what to be thankful for, be thankful for all the trouble you haven't had.

★ No one has inside information as good as the doctor's.

★ In this country every husband is free to do just what his wife pleases.

★ The best thing parents can spend on children is time—not money.

★ Where did you get the idea that swimming is good for the figure? Did you ever take a good look at a whale?

★ All of us work for the government. The trick is to get paid for it.

★ It's strange that the fellow who always wants the most had the least with which to buy it.

★ A man's hair is either parted or departed.

★ The hardest rupee to earn is the one you have already spent.

★ The person who leaves becomes the life of the party.

★ There is no special relation between what you want and what you need, and this makes selling interesting.

★ You can sleep on a matter before you decide, unless you have a competitor who doesn't need the sleep.

★ We like the person who tells us all the nice things about ourselves that we always knew.

★ Women keep a secret well, but sometimes it takes quite a few of them to do it.

★ Underprivileged: Not to have remote control for your colour television set.

★ It's always easier to have a courageous conviction after you know what the boss thinks.

★ It only takes one to start a quarrel, but it takes two to keep it up.

★ Nothing shocks most of us so much as finding that we may be wrong.

★ What a woman needs is a purse with a zipper on the bottom so she can find things quickly.

★ Many persons would like to do something for a living that doesn't involve work.

★ Experience is what helps you recognise the same mistake as you keep on making it.

★ After an election speech, the audience draws its own confusions.

★ Distance lends enchantment to the view, but not when you have a flat tire.

★ People who seldom speak aren't the only ones who don't say much.

★ Your head is like your pocketbook because it's not how it looks but what's inside that counts.

★ It's what the guests say after they say goodnight that counts.

★ Just because you blow your top, doesn't mean you have a dynamic personality.

★ Half the world doesn't know how many instalments the other half is behind.

★ Nothing is more trying than to have to neighbours buy things you can't afford.

★ A man needs a good yarn to pull the wool over his wife's eyes.

★ The world is composed of givers and takers. The takers may eat better, but the givers sleep better.

★ There's no fool like an old fool. You just can't beat experience.

★ Always borrow money from a pessimist—he never expects to be paid back.

★ Nothing stretches slacks like snacks.

★ Courage is what it takes to stand up and speak : courage is also what it takes to sit down and listen.

★ The condition a man is in can best be judged from what he takes two at a time—stairs or pills.

★ The best substitute for experience is being seventeen years old.

★ A reckless driver is one who passes you on the road, despite anything you can do.

★ A good listener is one who can give you his full attention without hearing a word you say.

★ The beginning of wisdom is silence. The second step is listening.

★ We understand the three most prolific writers of our time are Anonymous, Old Subscriber, and Steady Reader.

★ Variety may be the spice of life, but it's good old monotony that brings home the groceries.

★ Early to bed and early to rise—till you make enough cash to do otherwise!

★ Old gardeners never die; they just spade away.

★ The trouble with having a doctor who doesn't make house calls is you have to be in pretty good health to find out how sick you are.

★ What on earth will today's younger generation be able to tell their children they had to do without?

★ The trouble with people these days is that they want to reach the promised land without going through the wilderness.

★ When you begin to notice how much fun the young folks have, you are getting old.

★ Nowadays apples are so expensive, you might as well have the doctor.

★ If you look like your passport photo, you aren't well enough to travel.

★ If the knocking at the door is loud and long, it isn't opportunity, it's relatives.

★ When life knocks you to your knees, you're in a position to pray.

★ A person never realises how many friends he has until he rents a cottage at the beach.

★ There's a book that tells you where to go on your vacation. It's called a cheque book.

★ There's one advantage to the music the younger generation goes for today: nobody can whistle it.

★ Train up a child in the way he should go and when he gets older he will tell you how wrong you were.

★ People are peculiar—they want the front of the bus, the back of the church, and the middle of the road.

★ Don't be afraid of asking a dumb question! That's better than making a dumb mistake.

★ A good wife laughs at her husband's jokes, not because they are clever, but because she is.

★ A good test of your power of concentration is your ability to do your child's homework while he is watching television.

★ What is so simple even a small child can manipulate it? A grandparent.

★ When you sing your own praises, it's generally a solo.

★ It's surprising how long you remember a kind deed if you did it.

★ Most wallets wouldn't be so fat today if you took out the credit cards.

★ If you want more leisure, get to your appointments on time.

★ You can stand still and watch the world go by—and it certainly will.

★ You get on best when you don't try to tell people where to get off at.

★ No dream comes true until you wake up and go to work.

★ By the time you get the instalments paid, the luxury you bought is a necessity.

* You are young only once, and that excuse won't last forever.
* The world isn't getting smaller. The missiles just go farther.
* When business is slow, it's a good idea to give it a push.
* One thing about getting old is that you can sing in the bathroom while brushing your teeth.
* If people said what they thought, our conversation would be very brief.
* No opportunity is lost; the other fellow takes it.
* It isn't as hard to get the things you want as it is to keep from getting the things you don't want.
* You can't make trouble for others without a little of it rubbing off on you.
* The way to end an argument is to keep your mouth shut.
* Three square meals every day and you will soon be round.
* Unfortunately, laziness is never fatal.
* A swelled head always picks out an empty one to expand.
* Making money last is just as hard as making it first.
* A hammer may miss its mark, but a compliment never.
* Doing nothing gets pretty tiresome because you can't stop and rest.
* You may be a fine upstanding citizen, but it makes no difference on a slippery sidewalk.
* Some persons are poor listeners because it interferes with what they want to say.
* Getting rattled may be a sign that there is a screw loose somewhere.
* To get ahead you have to use a head.
* A girl loves a boy's voice when it has a ring in it.
* A loose nut can cause an auto accident, but so can a tight nut.
* Today no one is so poor that he has to live within his income.
* Don't worry too much about what people think, because they seldom do.
* The brain seldom wears out, probably because it's seldom overworked.
* It's easier for a woman to get her face lifted than it is for her husband to lift his when the bill comes in.

★ Some persons are born good and others have to make good.
★ In the grammatically correct home the wife says, "You shall" and the husband says, "I will."
★ A successful businessman keeps his head up and his overhead down.
★ None but the brave can afford the fair.
★ If you would like to be talked about, leave the party before the rest to.
★ We like the fellow who says he is going to make a long story short, and does.
★ We suppose a fat man dressed up is an illustration of spic and span.
★ Where do bad boys and girls go? Just about everywhere.
★ When both a speaker and an audience are confused, the speech is profound.
★ Why does a woman apologise when friends drop in unexpectedly and find the house looking like it usually does.
★ Most women have a skin they love to retouch.
★ June is the month when the bride who has never had a broom in her hand sweeps up the aisle.
★ Nothing makes time pass more quickly than an income-tax instalment every three months.
★ Money has wings and most of us see only the tail feathers.
★ Men are either born with conscience or marry them.
★ A saver grows rich by seeming poor. A spender grows poor by seeming rich.
★ The person who is ignorant can speak freely.
★ A civilised nation is one in which you decrease the death rate by disease and increase it by accident.
★ Fortunately, there are always enough crises in the world to help us keep our minds off our personal problems.
★ One way to find out what a woman really thinks of you is to marry her.
★ The reason a man dies suddenly in harness is the he has been working like a horse.
★ Freedom of speech is a great thing. It even permits some people to talk nonsense.
★ The fellow who laughs at his troubles never runs out of things at which

* Conversation without a touch of scandal gets very dull for most people.
* Ignorance combined with silence is sometimes mistaken for wisdom.
* The person who thinks before he speaks is silent most of the time.
* When a man doesn't believe today what he believed yesterday, how can he be so confident today knowing that tomorrow is coming?
* A fisherman is the only person who tells a lie with his arms stretched out.
* The most effective answer to an insult is silence.
* A person may be as young as he feels, but he is not often as important.
* You can't mind your own business if you haven't any mind and any business.
* There is no use in worrying about your old troubles when you know new ones will be coming along.
* It's surprising how soon a child learns how to train its parents.
* When some women promise to be on time, it carries a lot of wait.
* The person whose frequency is tight as a drum is seldom fit as a fiddle.
* The way to get in *Who's Who* is to know what's what.
* If you try to get something for nothing, you must be certain you don't end up getting nothing for something.
* People who live in glass houses have to answer the doorbell.
* The happiest moment in life is when the folks back of you in the movies finish their popcorn.
* Some persons don't know the difference between think for yourself and thinking of yourself.
* Worry takes as much time as work and pays less.
* Some people believe anything you tell them if you whisper it.
* As you grow older, you grow wiser, talk less, and say more.
* The owner of a candid camera generally takes the worst view of everything.
* It's almost impossible to keep your mind and your mouth open at the same time.

★ It's surprising how thoroughly you can be misinformed with a little reading.

★ You are not really ignorant until somebody finds it out.

★ A man is getting old when he starts letting his wife pick out his neckties.

★ One advantage in being poor is that your closest aren't full of old clothes and junk.

★ As a rule, a quitter isn't a very good beginner either.

★ Flattery is falsehood to all but the flattered.

★ The straight and narrow path never crosses Easy Street.

★ We have discovered spends that women used cosmetics in the middle ages. They still use them in the middle ages.

★ We still think having money a little tight teaches sobriety to spenders.

★ The Christmas cooing is followed by the January billing.

★ The family that isn't in debt today is underprivileged.

★ The Bible is such a great book that it survives all the translations made of it.

★ Some students burn the midnight oil in the transmission, instead of the lamp.

★ The person who has too much money for his own good easily finds friends to share his misfortune.

★ It is not sillier for the rich to think the poor are happy than for the poor to think the rich are.

★ The world's choice : Disarmament or Disbursement.

★ To be unhappily married requires a good income, and to be incompatible a couple must be rich.

★ Some persons never appeal to God unless they're getting licked.

★ A telephone isn't a vacuum cleaner, but some people can get a lot of dirt out of it.

★ No horse goes as fast as the money you bet on him.

★ All things come to him crosses the street without looking.

★ No matter how much money talks, most people don't find it boring.

★ A good idea can get very lonely in an empty head.

★ If you say you are less wise than you are, people will think you are wiser than you are.

★ If you know you don't know much, you know more than most people.

- ★ Some persons who are too proud to beg and too honest to steal, borrow and forget to pay.
- ★ The person who tells you his troubles keeps you from talking about yours.
- ★ The one thing it's easy to do these days is to get confused.
- ★ The grass on the other side of the fence may look greener, but it still has to be moved once a week.
- ★ Modern man looks ahead to going to the moon, but hesitates to move to the rear of the bus.
- ★ One reason a child must not suck his thumb is that he may need it someday.
- ★ One trouble in this country is that too many persons try to get something for nothing, and another trouble is that too many succeed.
- ★ All men are born free and equal and they stay that way up to the time they marry.
- ★ Every once in a while you see one of nature's big mistakes— a small mind with a large mouth.
- ★ The fellow who follows the horses generally finds the horses that follow the other horses.
- ★ Most of us who brag about what we are going to do tomorrow did the same thing yesterday.
- ★ Money can't buy happiness, but there are some mightily attractive substitutes.
- ★ Fun is expensive, and the older you get, the more expensive it is.
- ★ Most of us can't stand prosperity, and the way we spend money we won't have to.
- ★ Most of us make enough hay nowadays, but it's harder to stack it up.
- ★ It's a smart child who can ask questions his parents can answer.
- ★ There is nothing wrong with having nothing to say if you don't say it out loud.
- ★ You can knock the chip off the other person's shoulder simply by patting him on the back.
- ★ There are greater things in life than money, but the problem is convincing your life.
- ★ No one has more to learn than the person who knows everything.

★ Nothing takes the starch out of you like a strict diet.

★ Running into debt has its problems, but so does running into your creditors.

★ If at first you don't succeed, you are like the rest of us.

★ Keep smiling and it may look as if you are not smart enough to understand the world's problems.

★ The fellow who is a good sport has to lose to prove it.

★ When you blow your top, you will make the best speech you will ever regret.

★ If you get into deep water, the only safe course is to keep your mouth closed.

★ A person seldom loses anything by good manners, but some people don't even take a chance.

★ When you decide to know yourself, you may find the acquaintance isn't worth the effort.

★ A good idea can get very lonely in an empty head.

★ If you say you are less wise than you are, people will think you are wiser than you are.

★ If you know you don't know much, you know more than most people.

★ Some persons who are too proud to beg and too honest to steal, borrow and forget to pay.

★ The person who tells you his troubles keeps you from talking about yours.

★ The one thing that's easy to do these days is to get confused.

★ The grass on the other side of the fence may look greener, but it still has to be moved once a week.

★ Modern man looks ahead to going to the moon, but hesitates to move to the rear of the bus.

★ One reason a child must not suck his thumb is that he may need it someday.

★ One trouble in this country is that too many persons try to get something for nothing, and another trouble is that too many succeed.

★ All men are born free and equal and they stay that way up to the time they marry.

★ Every once in a while you see one of nature's big mistakes— a small mind with a large mouth.

★ The fellow who follows the horses generally finds the horses that follow the other horses.

* Most of us who brag about what we are going to do tomorrow did the same thing yesterday.
* Money can't buy happiness, but there are some mightily attractive substitutes.
* Fun is expensive, and the older you get, the more expensive it is.
* Most of us can't stand prosperity, and the way we spend money we won't have to.
* Most of us make enough hay nowadays, but it's harder to stack it up.
* It's a smart child who can ask questions his parents can answer.
* There is nothing wrong with having nothing to say if you don't say it out loud.
* You can knock the chip off the other person's shoulder simply by patting him on the back.
* There are greater things in life than money, but the problem is convincing your life.
* No one has more to learn than the person who knows everything.
* Nothing takes the starch out of you like a strict diet.
* Running into debt has its problems, but so does running into your creditors.
* If at first you don't succeed, you are like the rest of us.
* Keep smiling and it may look as if you are not smart enough to understand the world's problems.
* The fellow who is a good sport has to lose to prove it.
* When you blow your top, you will make the best speech you will ever regret.
* If you get into deep water, the only safe course is to keep your mouth closed.
* A person seldom loses anything by good manners, but some people don't even take a chance.
* When you decide to know yourself, you may find the acquaintance isn't worth the effort.
* A pessimist is a person who says all nations will share the atomic bomb.
* Sin is an old-fashioned word used to describe what is now called sophistication.
* You can fool all the people some of the time, but you can fool yourself all the time.

★ Half the world is always ready to tell the other half how to live.

★ You seldom are so busy that you can't stop and tell others how busy you are.

★ Most of us believe we are as good as we never were.

★ Money makes fools of famous people, but it also makes famous people of fools.

★ If you test a man's friendship by asking him to sign your note and he refuses, he is your friend.

★ One advantage about baldness is that it requires very little attention.

★ People who offer good advice always offer it in the big economy size.

★ Some persons think there is no difference between self-confidence and conceit.

★ If all the officers in a business agree, some of them aren't thinking.

★ As you grow older, you stand for more and fall for less.

★ A person has good manners if he is able to put up with bad ones in others.

★ When a person is always right, there is something wrong.

★ Everyone has fun at the fat man's expense.

★ Summer is the period when the children slam the doors they left open all winter.

★ The standard of living you can afford is the one you were on before you got your last raise.

★ Every husband knows how words can fail you.

★ An economist is a person who explains later how the thing he didn't expect was inevitable.

★ If the months were made shorter, we wouldn't have so much money left over at the end of the month.

★ Late to bed and early to rise makes you stupid rather than wise.

★ One way to reduce blood pressure is to live within you income.

★ Nothing is a better tranquiliser than a clear conscience.

★ The fellow who follows the advice "Know thyself" is pretty certain not to tell anyone about it.

★ Most of us enjoy defending a prejudice more than we do fighting for a principle.

* Punctuality is disappointing if no one is there to appreciate it.
* The next great advance is society will come when people become as speechless as they are thoughtless.
* The ant may be industrious, but it doesn't get on the front page as often as the butterfly.
* Truth in advertising : "The latest in antiques."
* On the sea of matrimony you have to expect occasional squalls.
* A bird in the hand is good, but remember it has wings.
* You can generally evade a difficult question with a long-winded answer.
* "A penny saved is a penny earned" was true up to the invention of the sales tax.
* If you want to win friends and influence people, you have to lose arguments.
* The person who takes him time often takes yours too.
* A scientist says life is the metabolic activity of protoplasm, but it seems worse than that on Monday morning.
* A lot of persons who say the boss is dumb would be out of job if the boss were any smarter.
* It's a great thing for a man to be married because he never has to worry about making up his mind.
* One way to make otherhappy is to leave them alone.
* He who hesitates is last.
* A fool and his money get to go places.
* Sometimes you find a person who knows how to live everyone's life expertly but his own.
* It is always easy to see the silver lining in the other person's cloud.
* If you think you know it all, you haven't been listening.
* A man who is on a wild-goose chase all his life never feathers much of a nest.
* It's strange how conscience may hurt when everything else seems pretty good.
* Nothing is as easy as it looks except spending money and getting into an argument.
* Experience is what helps you to recognise everyone's mistakes except your own.
* Schooldays are the happiest days parents have.

* Too many people determine what is right of wrong on the basis of which pays best.
* It's bad enough to make a fool of yourself, but it's worse if you don't know who did it.
* A hobby is something you go nuts about to keep from going nuts about what you are doing.
* A husband may read his wife like a book, but he can't shut her up that easily.
* Don't complain about getting old, because when you stop you are dead.
* Marriage is a mutual partnership if both parties know when to be mute.
* A generation ago most men who finished a hard day's work needed rest; now they need exercise.
* There are five thousands languages and dialects in the world, and money speaks all of them.
* Doctors say you should lie on the right side. We agree. If you must lie, always lie on the right side.
* Most of us say "no" to temptation once weakly.
* One trouble with the world is that there are too many clowns who aren't in the circus.
* Money doesn't make you happy, but it certainly quietens your nerves.
* A person who is overweight is living beyond his seams.
* An old master is an artist who could paint almost as well as those who have since copied his paintings.
* What the world needs is not people to rewrite the Bible, but people to reread it.
* Too many people think work is a good thing if it doesn't take up too much of your spare time.
* The person who always insists is on speaking his mind doesn't necessarily have one.
* Friendship is what makes you think almost as much of someone else as you do of yourself.
* There are a great many books now on how to live longer, but none on why.
* Public opinion is simply the private opinion of one person who makes enough noise to attract some converts.
* With some married couples the big difference of opinion is whether he earns too little or she spends too much.

* Obstacles are the terrible things you see when you take your eyes from the goal.
* Two can live as cheaply as one, and after marriage they do.
* Anger gets us into trouble because it makes the mouth move faster than the brain.
* A smart husband doesn't go home and complain about dinner, but takes his wife to a restaurant where they can both complain.
* Foresight is knowing when to close your mouth before someone suggests it.
* The only person more stupid than the person who thinks he knows it all is the person who argues with him.
* No man with money is short of cousins.
* A slip of the tongue will often cause greater damage than a slip of the foot.
* If you rest your chin on you hands when you think, it will help you to keep your mouth closed.
* Unless you can look interested when you are bored, you will never be a successful socially.
* A man who is always on the go often never gets there.
* Some people consider nothing is a luxury if they can afford it.
* Most of us spend a great deal of time just letting off esteem.
* It's good to have an open mind if you know what to let in.
* The faster a man runs into debt, the more he's best behind.
* It's impossible to push yourself ahead by patting yourself on the back.
* Sometimes we miss happiness by looking too far for things nearby.
* To reach a great height a person needs to have depth.
* Most girls want a spendthrift before they're married and a man who has saved his money after they're married.
* The fellow who slaps you on the back is probably trying to get you to cough up something.
* Think—and you will be very lonely.
* Always put of until tomorrow what you are going to make a mess of today.

★ When you get up tired without having been out the night before, you have reached middle age.

★ Most of us who are in debt could get along now if we could borrow from Peter to pay Paul without paying Paul.

★ The best business forecasting is done after the events occur.

★ It's one thing to guarantee free speech in a country, but it's another thing to guarantee its quality.

★ A man who agrees with everything you say needs to be watched.

★ It's difficult to take advice from some people when you know how much they need it themselves.

★ Posterity—what you write for after being turned down by publishers.—*George Ade*

★ Vacation is the period when you spend two weeks in an old shack without conveniences, so you can go back to your home with its comforts and complain.

★ A library has a sign, "Only how talk permitted," and we understood it when we saw the covers on the paperback books.

★ The way to be successful is to follow the advice you give others.

★ One of the first things man learns is to talk, and later in life he learns to keep still.

★ Blessed are the peacemakers—they will never be unemployed.

★ Believe only half you hear, but be sure it's the right half.

★ When a politician makes a ledge to spend more money, he always keeps it.

★ Most political candidates are more dandied than candid.

★ One way to get rid of weight is to leave it on the plate.

★ Some people say wild life is disappearing, but, from our observations, it is just moving to the cities.

★ In New York City they tear down thirty-five-storey shanties to make way for sixty-storey modern buildings.

★ Sometimes you wonder whether we should try to manage Europe, Asia, Africa and Latin America before we learn how to run one American city well.

★ Most people recognise their duty in time to avoid it.

★ Time is a great healer, but it's not much of a beauty parlour.

★ A hypocrite is a person who says he believes you when he knows you are not telling the truth.

★ The person who is always happy may be too lazy to complain.

★ Some prayers are so long because a person prays for more than he works for.

★ If you want to live on Easy Street, you have to save enough to buy a lot there.

★ A duty is a job you look forward to with distaste, perform with reluctance, and brag about ever after.

★ A small town is a place where a person with a black eye can't say he ran into a door.

★ Matrimony is a process by which the grocer acquires an account the florist had.

★ Worry is like a rocking chair : it given you something to do, but it won't get you any place.

★ If you punch a man in the nose when he calls you a fool, it may prove he was right.

Note: Use these punch lines. **Beware**: Don't get punch drunk.